CW00739593

The Tithe in Scripture: Being Chapters from "The Sacred Tenth" with a Revised Bibliography On Tithe-Paying and Systematic and Proportionate Giving

Henry Lansdell

This work has been selected by scholars as being culturally important, and is part of the knowledge base of civilization as we know it. This work was reproduced from the original artifact, and remains as true to the original work as possible. Therefore, you will see the original copyright references, library stamps (as most of these works have been housed in our most important libraries around the world), and other notations in the work.

This work is in the public domain in the United States of America, and possibly other nations. Within the United States, you may freely copy and distribute this work, as no entity (individual or corporate) has a copyright on the body of the work.

As a reproduction of a historical artifact, this work may contain missing or blurred pages, poor pictures, errant marks, etc. Scholars believe, and we concur, that this work is important enough to be preserved, reproduced, and made generally available to the public. We appreciate your support of the preservation process, and thank you for being an important part of keeping this knowledge alive and relevant.

BS
680
.T6
L28

PREFACE

THERE are, happily, throughout the world, many persons of all countries and in every clime who recognise that it is a religious and moral obligation to give ; and the publication of *The Sacred Tenth* has brought to the knowledge of the Author that, as in past ages, so now, many earnest people not only approve but practise the principle of setting aside from their incomes " not less than a tenth for God."

Some of these have suggested that inasmuch as the two volumes of *The Sacred Tenth* are not, and cannot be, within the reach of all, it is very desirable that there should be published apart, at least those portions thereof which are directly concerned with Holy Scripture.

Hence the appearance of the following chapters, to which is added a revised edition of the original bibliography with additions up to date. That these Scriptural studies may help many inquirers to " perceive and know " what is the mind and will of God respecting their giving, and that they may have " grace and power faithfully to perform the same," is the prayer and fervent desire of the Author.

HENRY LANSDELL, D.D.

MORDEN COLLEGE, BLACKHEATH, S.E.
Whitsuntide, 1908.

CONTENTS

Patriarchal

CHAPTER I

CAIN AND ABEL

Offering material things to God, 7.—Anciently connected with failure in tithe-paying, 7.—Bearing of the Septuagint on the rejection of Cain's offering, 8.—Sacrifices of Noah, Abram, and Jacob, 11 . . . . 7—12

CHAPTER II

ABRAM AND JACOB

Abram's tithe to Melchizedek, 13.—Tithing traced to Babylonia, 15.—Extent of Abram's tithes, 15.—Jacob's vow and its confirmation of tithe-paying, 17.—Scientific deduction from patriarchal tithing, 18.—Hypothesis for primeval origin of tithe-paying, 19.—Adam's sons presumably the first tithe-payers, 19.—Absence of written law, and silence of Genesis, no objection thereto, 21.—Pagan tithe-paying not learnt from Jewish Scriptures, 21 . . . . 13—22

Mosaic

CHAPTER III

ISRAEL'S THREE TITHES

Tithe-paying expressly enjoined in the Pentateuch, 24.—The first tithe, and observations thereon, 24.—Given by God to the Levites, 25.—The second, or festival, tithe ; its object, mode of payment, and personal benefit to the offerer, 26.—The third, or poor's, tithe, 30.—Not a substitute for second tithe, as witnessed by Tobit, Josephus, and others ; Maimonides to the contrary, notwithstanding, 32.—The third tithe, by modern comparison, not excessive, 34 . . . . . 23—36

3

CHAPTER IV
MOSAIC OFFERINGS

Old Testament
CHAPTER V
FROM JOSHUA TO SOLOMON

CHAPTER VI
BEFORE AND AFTER THE CAPTIVITY

Apocryphal

CHAPTER VII

TITHING IN THE APOCRYPHA

Talmudic

CHAPTER VIII

TALMUDIC TEACHING ON THE FIRST AND SECOND TITHES

CHAPTER IX

THE "DEMAI," OR DOUBTFUL TITHE

New Testament

CHAPTER X

CHRIST'S ATTITUDE AND EXAMPLE AS TO TITHING

THE TITHE IN SCRIPTURE

CHAPTER I

CAIN AND ABEL

Offerings to Jehovah, 7.—Cain's sin anciently connected with failure in tithe-paying, 7.—Bearing of the Septuagint on the rejection of Cain's offering, 8.—Sacrifices of Noah, Abram, and Jacob, 11.

THE picture-writings of Egypt, the cuneiform tablets of Babylonia, and early writers of Greece and Rome inform us that before the Bible was written, and apart therefrom, it was an almost universal practice among civilised nations for people to pay tithes to their gods ; but none tell us when, or where, the practice began, or who issued the law for its observance.

Our object therefore in this volume is to investigate what may be learned concerning tithe-paying from Holy Scripture, and from Jewish writings of the period between the Old and New Testaments.

If we begin by inquiring concerning tithe-paying from the book of Genesis, we naturally turn first to such passages as tell of the offering of material things to Jehovah. We find at least six persons who made such offerings—namely, Cain and Abel, Noah, Abram, Isaac, and Jacob; and we proceed to ask what we learn from them as to patriarchal or what is called pre-Mosaic tithe-paying.

1 Adversus Judæos, n. 2.

The rejection of Cain's offering was by very early Christian writers connected with tithing. Tertullian,[1] for instance, in the third century wrote that God rejected the sacrifice of Cain, because what he offered he did not rightly divide; following herein a Latin version of Genesis iv. 7, made from the Septuagint.* Some perhaps would call this reading a meaning into the text, rather than drawing one out of it: but before we thus judge let us see what can be said in its favour.

2 Gen. iv. 3-7.

Concerning Cain and Abel, our present Hebrew text [2] reads (as literally as I can translate it) thus :

" And it came to pass at the end of days Cain brought of the fruit of the ground a present to Jehovah. And Abel he also brought of the firstlings of his sheep and of their fat. And Jehovah looked favourably upon Abel and upon his present; but upon Cain and upon his present

* Clement of Rome also (*Ep. ad Corinth*. n. 4), who lived in the first century, and Irenæus, who wrote in the century following (*Adv. Hæres*. bk. iv. ch. 34), both quote the seventh verse according to the Septuagint reading. In the fourth century Hilary, Bishop of Poictiers, explaining Psalm cxviii., maintained that the receiving of tithes was a natural commandment from the beginning. So, again, in the twelfth century did Hugo, Abbot of St. Victor's, and Peter Comestor ; whilst, five centuries later, Grotius wrote upon this text that the sense, according to the Septuagint, was, that Cain either did not offer the best, or else that he gave a less proportion than the tenth, " which," he continues, " from the most ancient ages was the proportion due to God."

He did not look favourably. And it vexed Cain exceedingly, and his countenance fell. And Jehovah said to Cain, Wherefore did it vex thee, and wherefore did thy countenance fall? If thou wilt do well, shall not thy face be lifted up? but if thou wilt not do well, sin is couching at the door." *

But passing now to the Septuagint, or Greek, translation of Genesis, this sixth verse runs as follows :

" And the Lord God said to Cain, Wherefore didst thou become vexed, and wherefore did thy countenance fall? If thou didst rightly offer, but didst not rightly divide, didst thou not sin? Hold thy peace."

This Greek version, be it remembered, was made about three hundred years before the Christian era, from a Hebrew copy that must have been more than a thousand years older than the oldest Hebrew manuscript we possess now. This translation, moreover, was perfectly familiar to the writers of the New Testament. And if we may reverently picture the author of the Epistle to the Hebrews glancing over his Greek Bible before penning his chapter of Old Testament worthies, we should remember that he had before him these very words concerning Cain's not dividing rightly, when he wrote, " By faith Abel offered unto God a more abundant sacrifice (πλείονα θυσίαν) than Cain." [1]

[1] Heb. xi. 4.

Various suggestions, of course, are offered to show

* Professor Cheyne (*Encyclopædia Biblica*, I. 620, Article, "Cain") translates the sixth verse thus : "Why art thou wroth? and why is thy countenance fallen? Surely, if thou doest well, thou canst lift up thy head, and if thou doest not well, thy sin must cause it to fall ; from irritating words abstain, and thou take heed to thyself."

in what consisted the sin of Cain ; * but, be that as
it may, Abel is said to have offered "by faith."
Now faith has reference to obedience, which implies
that a previous command had been made known.
Where no law has been given there can be no
transgression ; and unless directions had been com-
municated to these two worshippers as to the
amount or proportion of their property to bring,
and if either was at liberty to offer as much or as
little as he pleased, then it is not easy to see why
Cain should by implication be blamed for bringing
less ; the occasion being, I take it, a farmer and a
grazier each bringing the firstfruits of his increase,
not so much as a propitiatory sacrifice (for we
are not told they had sinned), but rather as a
present or thankoffering to God in token of His
lordship over them—just as we may read [1] was
done from the earliest times in Egypt, and which
illustrates an almost universally accepted belief in
the ancient world, whether pagan or otherwise,
namely that it was not lawful to eat of the new
fruit until God's portion had been divided off from
the rest.†

*1 See Sacred
Tenth, p. 2.*

---

* A favourite one is that he brought no blood. But neither, in
after years, did an Israelite farmer bring blood, when he presented
his firstfruits to Jehovah, as commanded in Deuteronomy xxvi. 1—11.
The Hebrew word commonly used for a sacrifice with blood, זֶבַח
(*Zebach*), does not occur in the passage under consideration ; for both
Cain's fruits and Abel's firstlings are called by the same word, מִנְחָה
(*Minchah*), a present.

† In illustration of this I may observe that when on the Lower
Amur, in Eastern Siberia, I found among the Gilyaks—a people
quite untouched by Western ideas—the practice of taking some of
the blood of the first salmon caught during the season, and applying
it to the mouth of a rudely carved god, seated upon a fish's back, a

Thus far, it will be observed, no altar has been mentioned, nor is it said that Abel's firstlings were burnt. It is not until long afterwards that we find a sacrificial distinction mentioned between clean beasts and unclean;[1] and then it is we have on record the building of an altar on which clean animals and clean birds were consumed by fire.

[1] Gen. vii. 2.

In the case of Noah's sacrifice, with which we learn Jehovah was pleased, we have another instance of the presentation of a material offering to God, with the added accompaniments mentioned of an altar, fire, and a distinction between clean and unclean animals.

About three hundred years later we read that Abram twice built an altar,[2] and he called on the name of Jehovah, who appeared to him. At Mamre Abram did the same,[3] and later, when inquiring of Jehovah, he was expressly commanded to sacrifice a heifer, a she-goat, and a ram, each of them three years old, as well as a turtledove and a young pigeon.[4] We have yet another instance of Abraham building an altar when about to sacrifice his son, for whom, however, he ultimately substituted a ram.

[2] Gen. xii. 7-8.

[3] Gen. xiii. 18.

[4] Gen. xv. 9.

We read, likewise, of the patriarch Isaac, that he built an altar at Beersheba;[5] and the same may be

[5] Gen. xxvi. 25.

specimen of which, with fresh blood thereon, I was able to secure.— (Lansdell's *Through Siberia*, 3rd edition, p. 606, 1882). Also at Jerusalem, in 1890, I met the Rev. Charles T. Wilson, for many years resident in Palestine, who tells me that the Arabs wandering far east of the Jordan and out of reach of mission stations, fully recognize and habitually practise the duty of giving firstfruits of their increase.

1 Gen. xxxiii. 20. said of Jacob, at Shalem ;[1] whilst at Bethel we are told that Jacob at first set up a pillar, and poured

2 Gen. xxxiii. 18. oil thereon,[2] which act in after years he repeated,

3 Gen. xxxv. 1, 6, 14. adding to the oil a drink offering.[3]

If now we review the data thus far selected, we see the first recorded act of the first two of Eve's sons manifesting a sense of dependence on, or obligation to, the deity, by presenting to Jehovah the firstfruits of their increase ; and we see men of succeeding generations offering to God of the choicest of clean beasts, of clean birds, and fruits of the ground, as well as a drink offering and oil ; thus fully establishing, in connection with abundant information from pagan literature, that in all ages in the ancient world, men have thought it their duty to offer a portion of their substance to the divine Being.

CHAPTER II

ABRAM AND JACOB

WE now pass to the example of Abram, of
whom we read that the proportion of his
spoils that he devoted, was a tenth. Returning from
the slaughter of the kings with spoils of war, he was
met near Jerusalem by a kingly priest, Melchizedek,
who brought to Abram bread and wine, who blessed
Abram, who praised God for victory vouchsafed,
and to whom Abram offered a tenth of all.

Here, then, we have an instance of tithe-paying
which occurred (according to Ussher's chronology,
which is here followed throughout) about 1900 B.C.,
and this has ordinarily been regarded as the earliest
recorded instance of the payment of tithe.

But recent discoveries, transmitted to us by
students of cuneiform literature, have thrown a
flood of new light upon the land of Canaan before
it was peopled by the Israelites. Professor Sayce,

tracing the migration of Abram from Ur of the Chaldees, says in his *Patriarchal Palestine*:[1]

1 p. 66.

"Ur lay on the western side of the Euphrates in Southern Babylonia, where the mounds of Mugheir mark the site of the great temple that had been reared to the worship of the Moon-god long before the days of the Hebrew patriarch.

"Here Abram had married, and from hence he had gone forth with his father to seek a new home. Their first resting-place had been Harran in Mesopotamia. . . . Harran signified 'road' in the old language of Chaldæa, and for many ages the armies and merchants of Babylonia had halted there when making their way towards the Mediterranean. Like Ur, it was dedicated to the worship of Sin, the Moon-god; and its temple rivalled in fame and antiquity that of the Babylonian city, and had probably been founded by a Babylonian king.

"At Harran, therefore, Abram would still have been within the limits of Babylonian influence and culture, if not of Babylonian government as well. He would have found there the same religion as that which he had left behind him in his native city. . . .

"Even in Canaan Abram was not beyond the reach of Babylonian influence. . . . Babylonian armies had already penetrated to the shores of the Mediterranean, Palestine had been included within the bounds of a Babylonian empire, and Babylonian culture and religion had spread widely among the Canaanitish tribes. The cuneiform system of writing had made its way to Syria, and Babylonian literature had followed in its wake. Centuries had already passed since Sargon of Akkad had made himself master of the Mediterranean coast, and his son Naram-Sin had led his forces to the peninsula of Sinai."

Now if Babylonian culture and religion had thus spread to the Canaanites, it suggests a reason why the colony of Phœnicians from Tyre, who founded Carthage (say about 900 B.C.) were tithe-payers;[2]

2 See Sacred Tenth, p. 15.

and if Melchizedek may be regarded as a Canaanitish priest, then it would be as natural for him in his royal and priestly character to expect tithes from Abram as it was for Abram to pay them. Hence the professor, alluding to this incident, says : [1]

1 Patriarchal Religion, p. 175

" This offering of tithes was no new thing. In his Babylonian home Abram must have been familiar with the practice. The cuneiform inscriptions of Babylonia contain frequent references to it. It went back to the pre-Semitic age of Chaldæa, and the great temples of Babylonia were largely supported by the *esrâ* or tithe which was levied upon prince and peasant alike. That the god should receive a tenth of the good things which, it was believed, he had bestowed upon mankind was not considered to be asking too much. There are many tablets in the British Museum which are receipts for the payment of the tithe to the great temple of the sun-god at Sippara, in the time of Nebuchadnezzar and his successors. From one of them we learn that Belshazzar, even at the very moment when the Babylonian empire was falling from his father's hands, nevertheless found an opportunity for paying the tithe due from his sister."

A question may here be asked as to the extent of Abram's tithes : were they a tenth of all his spoils only, and so given voluntarily and specially on this particular occasion, or were they a tenth of all his income and something paid as a due?

Neither the Hebrew of Genesis nor the Greek of the Epistle to the Hebrews limits the word " all " to the spoils. In Hebrews vii. 4 the writer argues that Melchizedek was greater than Abram because Abram paid tithes to him. Now, when a man pays a tribute or due, we look upon the receiver as being, for the moment, superior to the giver; and the writer of the epistle adds that without contradiction the person less in dignity is blessed by the person who is greater in dignity.   Hence we conclude that the tenth paid by Abram was not merely an offering, which the patriarch was at liberty to render or to withhold as he pleased, but a payment of obligation.

This, too, appears the more likely because Abram by right of conquest might have claimed all that he captured from Chedorlaomer.   The king of Sodom, recognizing this, invites him to take the goods to himself.[1]   But Abram declines to take anything for himself, though, as a conqueror, he seems to have recognized that he had no jurisdiction over God's tenth ; and whilst surrendering his own claim to nine-tenths of the spoil, he acted as though he could not surrender God's.*

It seems, moreover, exceedingly probable that the priestly acts which Melchizedek performed for Abram were simply such as this priest-king would from time to time perform for any Canaanitish chief returning from a victorious expedition, as also perhaps when his people paid their tithes on ordinary occasions.   And since Abram often was dwelling within a day's journey of Salem (that is, Jerusalem), we need not at all conclude that this was either the first or the last occasion on which Abram paid a tenth of his increase to Melchizedek.   If the patriarch did so annually, it would be only in keeping with the practice of his Babylonian ancestors, and what we know was afterwards conceded by the Carthaginians to be due to their Phœnician priesthood.

1 Gen. xiv. 21.

* Compare *Gold and the Gospel*, p. 24.

This inference or supposition is strengthened to something like probability by consideration of the subsequent conduct of Abram's grandson Jacob, who, being about to undertake a journey, did what we know quite well was common among the Semites, the Greeks and Romans, and, indeed, is still practised : * he vowed a vow, and he said :

" If God will be with me, and will keep me in this way that I go, and will give me bread to eat, and raiment to put on, so that I come again to my father's house in peace; then shall the Lord be my God : and this stone which I have set up for a pillar, shall be God's house : and of all that Thou shalt give me I will surely give the tenth unto Thee."[1]   *1 Gen. xxviii. 20-22.*

Now it will be remembered that Abram lived till the boyhood of Jacob; that Jacob was brought up in the faith of his grandfather; and that at Bethel God confirmed to Jacob and his posterity all the promises He made to Abraham.   What, then, could be more natural than that Jacob should avow himself ready to practise Abraham's religious observances ? He promises to take the God of Abraham for his own God, to dedicate a certain place to His worship as did Abraham, and also to follow his grandfather's practice in dedicating to God a tenth of all he should receive.   But there are manifested certain points in Jacob's tithe-paying which we could not have certainly inferred in the offering of a tenth by Abram.[2]   *2 Gold and the Gospel, p. 28.*

For, first, Jacob's vow was, manifestly, to be con-

* I remember my Muhammadan interpreter in Bokhara telling me that before crossing the trans-Caspian desert he vowed that if God would bring him safely to Khiva, he would distribute bread to the prisoners in Bokhara. This vow he redeemed, and so was able to give me certain information I required about the structure of the prison.

2

tinued throughout his lifetime, and was not framed
for the occasion or the journey, only.

The second feature in Jacob's tenth differing from
that of his grandfather, is, that no part of Jacob's tithe
is mentioned as paid for the use of a priesthood.
We read no more of Melchizedek or of his successor; but, all the same, God's claim is not remitted
or abated, and Jacob's tithe-paying is presented to
us as an act of homage to God.

How, then, do these facts bear upon what may be
called the scientific aspect of the question?[1]

1 Sacred Tenth,
p. 37.

The prevalence of tithe-paying amongst ancient
nations, quite apart, so far as we see, from the
Bible, has, if possible, to be accounted for. If it
was originally left to every man to give for religious
purposes merely according to his own inclination—
that is, as much or as little as he pleased—then how
should so many peoples have hit upon a tenth for
God's portion, rather than a fifth, or a fifteenth, or
any other? Does not the universality of this proportion point to a time when the ancestors of those
nations lived together, and so derived the custom
from a common source?

No profane author, and no account or tradition
known to us in any country, professes to give that
origin, nor does the Bible do so in express terms.
Can we, then, frame any hypothesis that would
account for the facts before us?

Most men, presumably, will allow that sacrifice
was not a human invention, but a divine institution
appointed by God. And if God appointed also that
some things were acceptable to Him as "clean," and

others not so, is it reasonable to suppose that He
would have omitted directions about the quantity, or
proportion in which such things should be offered?

If, then, we may venture the hypothesis that God
from the beginning taught Adam that it was the
duty of man to render a portion of his increase to his
Maker, and that that portion was to be not less than
a tenth, then we shall see that the facts recorded
in Genesis not only do not contradict such a supposition, but corroborate and strengthen it.

The Septuagint version, then, would show an
instance of covetousness in the person of Cain, as
does the Acts of the Apostles in the persons of
Ananias and Sapphira, each pretending to offer
more than was really given, each attempting to
deceive the Almighty, and thus, in New Testament
language, lying to the Holy Ghost.[1]   [1] Acts v. 3.

In accord with this theory, also, Abel's fuller sacrifice was accepted; and so sacrifice and tithe-paying
may be presumed to have continued all along the
centuries to the days of Noah. Then, when his
descendants built cities in Babylonia and afterwards
became scattered, they would naturally take with
them, among other primeval customs and traditions,
the offering of sacrifice and tithe-paying. And thus
would be accounted for, only a few centuries later,
the existence of these customs as recorded in
cuneiform literature on the tablets we possess, as
well as the information given us about tithe-paying
in the literatures of Egypt, Greece, and Rome.

It is not pretended that this hypothesis *must* be
true, or that no other can be advanced; but mean-

while I am among those who think that it meets the facts of the case, but who hold themselves ready to examine another theory if forthcoming.*

It may be objected, of course, that we do not read in Genesis of a law for the payment of a tenth; which is no proof, however, that no such law had been given, seeing there existed various laws in primeval times of which we have no written evidence now. Do any, for instance, doubt that there was, from the beginning, a law against murder, for breaking of which Cain was punished; or against adultery, in keeping with which Judah said of Tamar, "Bring her forth and let her be burnt"?[1] Similarly, it is possible that tithe-paying may have been among the " commandments and the statutes and the laws " of God which Abraham is praised for keeping, but which have not come down to us in writing.[2]

Or, again, if it be urged that tithes are not even mentioned until the days of Abram and so were till then unknown, it is easy to point to persons and things which we feel sure must have existed long before they are mentioned in the order of events recorded in Genesis.

1 Gen. xxxviii. 24.

2 Gen. xxvi. 5.

* After this chapter was written, my attention was called to Professor Cheyne's articles on " Cain " and " Abraham " in the *Ency-clopædia Biblica* (vol. i. 23. 260), which would make the accounts of these two persons of later origin by several centuries than is generally received. But this does not greatly affect the main purpose of my argument. Moreover, if Professor Petrie is right in telling us that from three to four thousand years or more before Christianity appeared, the ancient Egyptians repudiated, before the judgment of Osiris, sins such as "cutting short the rations of the temples," "diminishing the offerings of the gods" and stealing their property, then the story of Cain, as interpreted from the reading of the Septuagint, has a striking resemblance thereto, and is thereby rendered more credible.

Melchizedek, for instance, is the first man in the Bible called a priest; Amraphel of Shinar is the first man called a king,[1] and Abram the first called a prophet. But when these three lived, men had been on the earth for a great many years; and are we to suppose that mankind had lived century after century without priests, kings, and prophets? ^{1 Gen. xiv. 1.}

Again, Noah is the first who is expressly called a " righteous man," and Abram is the first who is said to have "believed in God"; yet we know that before these, Abel and Enoch were both righteous, and also believed in God. Once more : the human race had been on the earth, according to the received chronology, about a thousand years before we read of musical instruments;[2] and it was a thousand years later still when Abraham weighed shekels of silver as payment. But he would be a bold man who would affirm that before these dates, respectively, mankind possessed neither music nor money! ^{2 Gen. iv. 21.}

The mere omission, therefore, of the definite mention of a law concerning tithe-giving, in the less than a dozen chapters given to us in Genesis concerning the early history of the world, is no proof or presumption whatever that such a law did not exist.

As another objection to our hypothesis, it has been suggested that the pagan nations of antiquity may have learned the practice of tithe-paying from the Jews. But can this suggestion be supported by one tittle of evidence? Can a single passage be adduced from any Greek or Roman classic to confirm such an idea? Is there the remotest reason to suppose that the Greeks before the Trojan war, or the Romans in the days of Romulus, knew anything about the Jews, or, even if they did, that they thought of them otherwise than with contempt?

Nor does the suggestion much help us that the Phœnicians of Tyre might have learned tithe-giving from Abram before they colonized Carthage, because it has been all but demonstrated that tithes were paid in Babylonia before Abram was born, so that for the origin of the practice we are sent further back, seemingly, than 2000 B.C.

In face, therefore, of the overwhelming probability that a tenth was the proportion of increase originally required by God from man, I, for one, prefer to believe that sacrifice and tithe-paying existed and continued from the beginning, and, as men dispersed, were taken throughout the ancient world.

How far the practice afterwards became modified among pagan nations it is not my purpose to inquire here, but rather to follow up tithe-paying as brought out of Babylonia by Abram, as observed by his grandson Jacob, and afterwards adopted amongst Jacob's descendants, the children of Israel.

CHAPTER III

ISRAEL'S THREE TITHES

WE have now reached a higher platform, which suggests a change of venue, or, at all events, the looking at our subject from a different standpoint.

Thus far we have heard of the custom of tithe-paying throughout the ancient world, and have argued, from the universality of the observance, that there was probably some primitive law which enjoined it. What that law was, who enjoined it, or when, neither secular literature nor ancient monuments inform us; nor does the book of Genesis make these points clear to demonstration.

If, however, we may assume that God directed from the first that a tenth of man's increase would be a fitting proportion to render to Himself, as the great Lord of all, then, not only do we find nothing in Genesis to conflict with a theory of this kind, but, on the contrary, we see several passages connected with patriarchal religion that seem to confirm such an idea, and to make the assumption highly probable.

When, moreover, we come to other books of the Pentateuch, we are brought face to face with written laws which distinctly deal with tithe payments, not indeed as a new institution, but as regulated and adapted to a new form of government on which was based the Jewish polity.

1 ch. xxvii. 30-33.   Thus we read in Leviticus : [1]

"And all the tithe of the land, whether of the seed of the land, or of the fruit of the tree, is the Lord's: it is holy unto the Lord. And if a man will redeem aught of his tithe, he shall add unto it the fifth part thereof. And all the tithe of the herd or the flock, whatsoever passeth under the rod, the tenth shall be holy unto the Lord. He shall not search whether it be good or bad, neither shall he change it : and if he change it at all, then both it and that for which it is changed shall be holy ; it shall not be redeemed."

From this passage we learn :

That a tenth of the produce of the land, whether of seed or fruit, was claimed by God, and was to be regarded as holy (or set apart) for Him.

That if the offerer wished to retain this tenth of seed or fruit, he might do so by paying its value, and adding thereto one-fifth.

That every tenth calf and lamb also (that is, increase of the herd or flock) was to be set apart for Jehovah.

That this form of animal tithe might not be

redeemed, nor the animals exchanged: but if an owner, notwithstanding, presumed to change a tithe animal, then both the tithe animal* and that for which it was exchanged were to be forfeited, and set apart for Jehovah.

From the book of Numbers [1] we learn that the tithe just mentioned, though claimed by Jehovah Himself, was given by Him to the Levites. Thus:

1 ch. xviii. 21-4.

"And unto the children of Levi, behold, I have given all the tithe in Israel for an inheritance, in return for their service which they serve, even the service of the tent of meeting. And henceforth the children of Israel shall not come nigh the tent of meeting, lest they bear sin, and die. But the Levites shall do the service of the tent of meeting, and they shall bear their iniquity: it shall be a statute for ever throughout your generations, and among the children of Israel they shall have no inheritance. For the tithe of the children of Israel, which they offer as a heave offering unto the Lord, I have given to the Levites for an inheritance."

Hence this first, or Lord's tithe, is known also as the Levites' tithe, concerning which it may be convenient here to notice:

---

* The manner of tithing, as described by Maimonides, was this: "He [the owner] gathers all the lambs and all the calves into a field, and makes a little door to it, so that two *cannot* go out at once ; and he places their dams without, and they bleat, so that the lambs hear their voice, and go out of the fold to meet them, as it is said, *whatsoever passeth under the rod*: for it must pass of itself, and not be brought out by his hand ; and when they go out of the fold, one after another, he begins and counts them with the rod: one, two, three, four, five, six, seven, eight, nine, and the tenth that goes out, whether male or female, whether perfect or blemished, he marks it with a red mark, and says, 'This is the tithe.'" (*Hilchot Becorot*, c. 6, sect. 1 ; from Gill's *Exposition*, on Lev. xxvii. 32.)

That from this tithing no produce of land, or increase of herd or flock, is excepted.

That the offerer had no voice in its disposal.

That though it was called a heave offering, the offerer did not receive any of it back again.

That this tithe was not an amount that might be diminished, or an alms that the owner might render or not as he pleased, but a divine claim, the withholding of which was regarded by God as dishonesty.[1]

1 Mal. iii. 8.

It may further be noted concerning this first tithe that the Levites, to whom it was given by God, were required by Him to render a tenth of what they received as a heave offering to Jehovah, and to pay it to Aaron the priest.[2]

2 Num. xviii. 26-8.

"When ye take of the children of Israel the tithe which I have given you from them for your inheritance, then ye shall offer up a heave offering of it for the Lord, a tithe of the tithe. And your heave offering shall be reckoned unto you, as though it were the corn of the threshing-floor, and as the fulness of the winepress. Thus ye also shall offer a heave offering unto the Lord of all your tithes, which ye receive of the children of Israel; and thereof ye shall give the Lord's heave offering to Aaron the priest."

We now proceed to a second tithe, which reads thus :[3]

3 Deut. xiv. 22-7.

"Thou shalt surely tithe all the increase of thy seed, that which cometh forth of the field year by year. And thou shalt eat before the Lord thy God, in the place which He shall choose to cause His name to dwell there, the tithe of thy corn, of thy wine, and of thine oil, and the firstlings of thy herd and of thy flock; that thou mayest learn to fear the Lord thy God always. And if the way be too long for thee, so that thou art not able to carry it, because the place is too far from thee, which the Lord thy God shall choose to set His name there, when the Lord thy God shall bless thee: then shalt thou turn it into money, and bind up the money in thine hand, and shalt go unto the place which the Lord thy God shall choose: and thou shalt bestow the money for whatsoever thy soul desireth, for oxen, or for sheep, or for wine, or for strong drink, or for whatsoever thy soul asketh of thee: and thou shalt eat there before the Lord thy God, and thou shalt rejoice, thou and thy household: and the Levite that is within thy gates."

Concerning the second tithe, we seem to learn:

That it consisted of the yearly increase of the land.

That it was to be eaten by the offerer, his household, and the Levite, with firstlings of herd and flock, but only at the appointed place of worship.

The object of this was that Israel might always fear Jehovah.

This tithe might be converted at home into money, to be expended at the capital for sacrifices and feasting.

The tithe-payer was to eat and rejoice before God.

The due payment of this second tithe involved a stay of at least a week each at the Passover and the Feast of Tabernacles, as well as a shorter period at the Feast of Weeks.[1]

1 Deut. xvi. 3, 13, 16.

It will help us better to understand this second, or festival tithe, as it is sometimes called, if we consider the end it was to serve. All the males in Israel (with their families, if they chose) were to assemble at the sanctuary three times a year for the worship of God.[1]

1 Deut. xii. 6-7.

"And thither ye shall bring your burnt offerings, and your sacrifices, and your tithes, and the heave offerings of your hand, and your vows, and your freewill offerings, and the firstlings of your herd and of your flock : and there ye shall eat before the Lord your God, and ye shall rejoice in all that ye put your hand unto, ye and your households."

The primary end, therefore, of the festivals was to foster religious principles and to furnish a time and place for social observances and the offering of sacrifices, all being done in recognition of God's bounty, and as acts of fealty and worship to Him. Now, in all nations, the main idea of a sacrifice has been that of a meal offered to a deity.[2] In some cases the meal was made over entirely to the god ; but more commonly the sacrifice was a feast, of which the god and the worshippers were supposed to partake together. In other words, the offering rendered, whether animal or vegetable, was sometimes wholly burnt ; at others, was consumed partly by fire and partly by the priest ; or, once more, part was burnt, part was taken by the priest, and a part returned to the offerer.

2 Encyclopædia Britannica, 9th ed., " Sacrifice," by W. Robertson Smith, vol. xxi. 132.

So, if an Israelite sinned, his appointed way to forgiveness was by sacrifice ; and if he had vows to redeem, or thanksgivings to make, all involved the presentation of sacrifice. But this and other sacrifices were not to be offered in just any place the worshipper chose,[3] but must be taken to the ecclesiastical capital, such as was afterwards estab-

3 Deut. xii. 17-18.

lished at the resting-places of the Ark, as in Shiloh, and in Jerusalem.

Speaking generally, the Jewish sacrifices partook more or less of the nature of expiation (for sin committed), of dedication (when seeking a favour), or of thanksgiving (for favour received); and according to the intention of the offerer was the kind of sacrifice presented.

In the case of the burnt offering proper, the priest took the skin, but all else was consumed by fire.[1] [1 Lev. vii. 8.] In the case of the sin offering, the trespass offering, and the meat (or meal) offering, that which was not burnt was for the officiating priest, or the priests generally;[2] whilst, in the case of the peace offering, [2 Lev. v. 2-10, vii. 6-10.] the breast and right shoulder only belonged to the priests, and the remainder might be consumed by the offerer.*

Thus the Israelite would have the opportunity of eating and rejoicing before God, and feasting with his household; and the second, or festival, tithe, was intended to furnish the means for doing this.

Furthermore, if the first and second tithes be compared, it will be seen, by way of distinction, that whereas the offerer had no voice whatever in

* I remember how these distinctions were practically brought home to my mind in India at Jaipur, where, at the daily sacrifice, I saw a goat decapitated before a Hindu altar. The head was placed on the altar, curtains were drawn, and the god was supposed to be left to partake of the meal in some mysterious way. Again, in Calcutta, as I approached the temple of Kali, I saw a man carrying the headless carcase of a goat, which he had just offered in sacrifice, the head having been taken by the priest, and the offerer being at liberty to dispose of the carcase as he pleased.

the disposal of the first tithe, the disposal of the second tithe was largely in his own hands; and that whereas the offerer did not receive again any portion for himself of the first tithe, he might receive in some cases the greater part of the second tithe for his own use, or purposes, as well as for the enjoyment of others.

We now come to a third tithe:[1]

*1 Deut. xiv.
28-9.*

"At the end of every three years thou shalt bring forth all the tithe of thine increase in the same year, and shalt lay it up within thy gates; and the Levite, because he hath no portion nor inheritance with thee, and the stranger, and the fatherless, and the widow, which are within thy gates, shall come, and shall eat and be satisfied; that the Lord thy God may bless thee in all the work of thine hand which thou doest."

This seems to teach that:

A tenth of every third year's increase was to be laid up at home.

This tenth was to be shared by the local Levite, the stranger, the fatherless, and the widow.

The object of this tithe was, that Jehovah might bless the work of the tithe-payer's hands.

Some think this was not a third tithe, but a triennial substitute for the second tithe, so that in the third, and again the sixth, years (as well as the seventh year, when the land was not to be cultivated), the Israelite would not take the second, or festival, tithe to the sanctuary, but would dispose of it among the poor at home.

Perhaps this view may have been in part suggested by the Septuagint, which varies the punctuation, and reads: "After three years thou shalt bring forth all the tithe of thine increase. In that year thou shalt lay it up in thy cities."[1] *

[1] Deut. xiv. 27.

Selden and Michaelis also argue in the same direction, saying that a third tithe would be an excessive demand upon the income of a man who had already expended two-tenths of his increase.[2]

[2] McClintock and Strong's Cyclopædia, vol. x. p. 434.

Peake likewise says : "It may be urged that it is not probable that a double tribute should be exacted from the crops." And again : "Nor is it probable that a tax of nearly one-fifth of the whole produce should be imposed on the farmers."[3]

[3] Article "Tithe," in Hastings' Dictionary of the Bible, I. p. 780.

On the other hand, as opposed to these conjectures, it may be observed :

That the Hebrew text nowhere says explicitly that the third tithe should be substituted for the second.

The injunction is several times repeated that every male should go up to the festivals yearly ; but neither the third, sixth, seventh, or any other year is excepted.†

* In support of this opinion may be quoted the words of Maimonides : "On the third and sixth years from the sabbatical year, after they have separated the first tithe, they separate from what remains another tithe, and give it to the poor, and it is called the poor's tithe ; and not on those two years is the second tithe, but the poor's tithe."—Gill on Deut. xiv. 28 ; Maimonides, *Hilchot Mattanot Anayim*, c. 6, sect. 4. See also *Speaker's Commentary* on Deut. xiv. 28-9, and McClintock and Strong's *Cyclopædia*, vol. x. p. 433.

† Some (and Professor Driver[4] among them) have supposed that, as the land was not to be sown in the seventh year, no tithe would be paid (McClintock and Strong, vol. x. p. 435). But if so, how were the Levites during that year to live, unless a double or treble tithe was to be paid in the sixth year ? And this the law had already provided for. "If ye shall say, What shall we eat the seventh year ? behold we shall not sow, nor gather in our increase. Then I will command My blessing upon you in the sixth year, and it shall bring forth fruit for three years," etc. (Lev. xxv. 20-2).

[4] International Critical Commentary, Deuteronomy, p. 168.

Besides, not going up to the festivals on the third, sixth, and seventh years would be attended with a further and practical difficulty : for if a man had sinned after returning, say, from the last feast of the fifth year, he would, under normal circumstances, be deprived of the opportunity of offering a sacrifice of expiation at the sanctuary until after an interval of two years.

Moreover, we have at least three witnesses of prominent rank for the third tithe being an addition to, and not a substitute for, the second tithe. The author of Tobit, for instance, when stating how he walked in the ways of truth and righteousness, notwithstanding the falling away of his father's family from God's command to sacrifice at Jerusalem, makes his subject say :

"I alone went often to Jerusalem at the feasts, as it hath been ordained unto all Israel by an everlasting decree, having the firstfruits and the tenths of mine increase, and that which was first shorn ; and I gave them at the altar to the priests, the sons of Aaron. The tenth part of all mine increase I gave to the sons of Levi, who ministered at Jerusalem : and the second tenth part I sold away, and went, and spent it each year at Jerusalem : and the third I gave unto them for whom it was meet, as Deborah my father's mother had commanded me." [1]

1 Tobit i. 6-8.

The foregoing quotation is the revised English version from the Vatican codex ; but the reading of the Sinaitic codex is still more noteworthy.*

* I translate this passage as follows :
" Having the firstfruits, and the firstborn and the tithes of cattle, and the first shearing of the sheep, I proceeded to Jerusalem, and I gave them to the priests, the sons of Aaron, at the altar ; and the

Again, Josephus is quite clear as to a third tithe. He writes:

"Beside those two tithes which I have already said you are to pay every year, the one for the Levites, the other for the festivals, you are to bring every third year a tithe to be distributed to those that want ; to women also that are widows, and to children that are orphans." [1]

1 Josephus, Antiquities, bk. iv.

After Josephus we have the testimony of Jerome, who, like the preceding two witnesses, lived in Palestine. He says one tithe was given to the Levites, out of which they gave a tenth to the priests ; a second tithe was applied to festival purposes, and a third was given to the poor.[2] And so, evidently, Chrysostom understood, for he preaches : "What, then, did they [the Jews] give? A tenth of all their possessions, and another tenth, and after this a third [tenth]," etc.[3]

2 Commentary on Ezek. xlv. i. 565, quoted in McClintock and Strong, x. 434.

3 Homily lxiv. on Matt. xx. 27.

Once more, for a modern opinion to the same purpose, may be instanced that of Dr. Pusey, late Regius Professor of Hebrew at Oxford, who, preaching on Ash Wednesday, at St. Paul's, Knightsbridge, is quoted thus :

The Pharisee "paid tithes of all which he possessed: a double tithe, you will recollect, one for God's priests, the tenth of the wine, and of the corn, and of olive, and pomegranate, and the other fruit trees to the sons of Levi ministering in Jerusalem.

"And the second tithe I sold away for money during six years, and I used to go every year and spend it in Jerusalem. And I gave them [*i.e.* the tithes] to the orphans, and to the widows, and to the strangers living among the children of Israel. I brought in and I gave [the tithes] to them in the third year, and we ate them according to the ordinance ordained concerning them in the law of Moses, and according to the commandments which Deborah, the mother of Ananeel our father, commanded.

other for the sacrifices, and yet another every third year for the poor : 4*s*. 8*d*. in the pound he anyhow gave to God, not, as our custom is, underrating property for the poor-rate, but a good 4*s*. 8*d*. in the pound on the average of the three years." [1]

1 Pearson, Systematic Bene-ficence, p. 11.

In fact, I can find no authority in favour of this supposed triennial substitution of the third tithe for the second, until the twelfth century, when Mai-monides says that the third and sixth years' second tithe was shared between the poor and the Levites, *i.e.* that there was no third tithe.[2] But even then we have a contemporary rabbi of the same century (Aben Ezra) who says : "This was a third tithe, and did not excuse the second tithe."[3]

2 De Jur. Paup. vi. 4, quoted in McClintock and Strong, x. p. 434.

3 See Gill on Deut. iv. 28.

The reader, therefore, will judge concerning the plain statement of the law, supported by what we have seen was thought right by the author of the book of Tobit in perhaps the third century before Christ ; and also at the time of Josephus (two or three centuries later, and when tithe-paying was still practised),[4] together with the testimony of Jerome (who lived in Palestine four centuries later, and may be presumed to have known how his contem-poraries, at least among the Samaritans, were paying their tithes,) whether all this is not more likely to be true than a statement such as that of Maimonides, who, though buried in Palestine, yet flourished in Spain, but not until a thousand years after the Jewish nation had been dispersed.

4 See Sacred Tenth, pp. 79, 106.

As for the objection that a third tithe would be an excessive demand upon income, the late Sir Monier Williams, Professor of Sanskrit at Oxford, having referred me to passages of Sanskrit law, especially the code of Manu, the oldest compendium of the laws of the Brahmans, pointed out that the usual proportion of produce taken by the king was a sixth part (as we have seen was the case in Egypt),[1] but that in times of necessity he might take one-fourth of the crop.[2]

We may remember also that, in the time of the Maccabees, the inhabitants of Judea seem to have been taxed to the extent of one-third of their seed and half of their fruit.[3]

For modern illustrations I would observe, that on my first visit to Bokhara, in 1882, I asked about taxes, and received widely divergent answers in different parts of the Khanate. At one place they said that out of ten batmans of harvest they paid eight (or four-fifths) for taxes; and at another, four (or a half); and that, as a matter of fact, the *beks* took more and more, and as much as they pleased.[4]

Again, in 1894, when travelling through most of the large towns of Italy, I was told more than once that the taxes then being levied upon the people amounted to at least 20 per cent. of their incomes. Given, then, a conscientious Italian paying 20 per cent. of his income to the State, and, as expected by the Council of Trent,[5] another tithe, or 10 per cent., to his church, and these demands, united, would be a heavier claim upon income than the three tithes of the law. Moreover, if Josephus could enjoin the Jews to pay three tithes for their own religion, when they were paying also taxes to the Romans, much more might the Mosaic law

[1] See Sacred Tenth, p. 8.
[2] Monier Williams, Indian Wisdom, p. 264.
[3] 1 Maccabees, x. 30.
[4] Lansdell's Russian Central Asia, vol. ii. p. 187.
[5] Session xxv. ch. 12.

require three tithes under the theocracy, especially as the payment of these procured to the Israelite not a few of the judicial, educational, and social benefits for which other nations now pay taxes.

It would seem, then, that the Mosaic law enjoined upon the Israelite to pay yearly, in connection with his religion, two-tenths, and, at the end of three years, a third tenth, of his income.

CHAPTER IV

MOSAIC OFFERINGS

BESIDES three tithes, properly so-called, the Pentateuch imposed other fixed claims, both annual and occasional. Thus the Israelite was commanded :

" When ye reap the harvest of your land, thou shalt not wholly reap the corners of thy field, neither shalt thou gather the gleaning of thy harvest. And thou shalt not glean thy vineyard, neither shalt thou gather the fallen fruit of thy vineyard ; thou shalt leave them for the poor and for the stranger." [1]

[1] Lev. xix. 9-10.

Again :

" When thou reapest thine harvest in thy field, and hast forgot a sheaf in the field, thou shalt not go again to fetch it : it shall be for the stranger, for the fatherless, and for the widow : that the Lord thy God may bless thee in all the work of thine hands. When thou beatest thine olive tree, thou shall not go over the boughs again. . . . When thou gatherest the grapes of thy vineyard, thou shalt not

37

glean it after thee; it shall be for the stranger, for the fatherless, and for the widow." [1]

1 Deut. xxiv. 19-21.

From the foregoing we learn that, at the time of fruit-gathering, the owner was to leave for the needy, fallen fruit, overlooked olives, and small bunches of grapes; whilst in the harvest field he was not to care for forgotten bundles nor gleanings (that is, ears of corn dropped from the hands of the reaper); and the corners of his fields he was not even to cut.

How large the corners thus left were to be, the Mosaic law does not specify; but as a matter of practice we learn, in later years, from a chapter on "the corner" in the *Mishna*, that "they do not leave less than a sixtieth part" of the whole.[2]

2 Gill's Exposition of O. and N. T., Lev. xix.9.

Another annual claim upon the Israelite was that of his firstfruits; and although the law, again, does not define the amount of the offering, it is instructive to notice how Maimonides asks concerning the quantity to be brought, " What measure do the wise men set?" which he answers, saying, " A good eye [or a bountiful man] brings one of forty; a middling one [one that is neither liberal nor niggardly] brings one of fifty [or the fiftieth part]; and an evil one [a covetous man] one of sixty [or the sixtieth part]; but never less than that."[3]   Another authority, referring to the *Mishna* and its chapter on firstfruits, names one-fiftieth of the produce.[4]

3 Gill on Exod. xxii. 29.

4 See McClintock and Strong's Cyclopædia, article " Tithe," vol. x. p. 434.

But besides the firstfruits to be offered annually, the law enjoined certain charges to be paid occasionally.   Thus:

" Sanctify unto Me all the firstborn, whatsoever openeth

the womb among the children of Israel, both of man and of beast ; it is Mine."

Again :

"The firstborn of thy sons shalt thou give unto Me. Likewise shalt thou do with thine oxen, and with thy sheep : seven days it shall be with its dam ; on the eighth day thou shalt give it Me." [1]

1 Exod. xiii. xxii. 29-30.

The firstborn of man was to be redeemed by payment of five shekels ; * and the firstlings of unclean animals were to be redeemed also. The firstling, however, of a cow, a sheep, or a goat might not be redeemed ; but it was brought to the altar, and the flesh, after being offered to God, became the property of the priest.[2]

2 Deut. xviii. 16-17.

Another fixed charge was made at the time of the census in the wilderness to the amount of half a shekel. The rich were not to give more, nor the poor less.[3] Also the law prescribed that when the Israelite should plant a fruit tree, the fruit for three years was to be regarded as unclean, and not to be eaten ; whilst in the fourth year the fruit was to be set apart for giving praise to Jehovah.[4]

3 Exod. xxx. 11-14.

4 Lev. xix. 23-24.

* This is still observed, apparently, among modern Jews in Lemberg. Mr. Israel Sunlight, an ex-rabbi of my acquaintance (and who was kind enough to read over what I have hereafter written about Talmudic teaching on tithes), writes thus : "At the beginning of the month I was invited to be present at a unique ceremony, the redeeming of the firstborn" ; and he continues, in short, as follows : The parents present the child to the *cohen* (or priest), who takes it in his arms, and then asks them whether they wish him to keep the child, or whether they would rather redeem it for the sum of five shekels (about twelve shillings). The parents, of course, take the latter alternative, and pay down the redemption money : whereupon the priest pronounces his blessing upon the child, and hands it back to its parents (*Jewish Missionary Intelligencer*, March, 1903, p. 43).

Moreover, the seventh year was to be a year of release, when every creditor was to refrain from enforcing re-payment for that which he had lent to his neighbour :

"Beware that there be not a base thought in thine heart, saying, The seventh year, the year of release, is at hand ; and thine eye be evil against thy poor brother, and thou give him nought : and he cry unto the Lord against thee, and it be sin unto thee." [1]

1 Deut. xv. 1-2, 9.

Such, then, were the fixed deductions, annual or occasional, laid by the Mosaic law upon an Israelite's increase, the discharge of which was a duty and the withholding a sin.

Besides the foregoing, it was enjoined for the Feast of Weeks :

"Thou shalt keep the feast of weeks unto the Lord thy God with a tribute of a freewill offering of thine hand, which thou shalt give, according as the Lord thy God blesseth thee : and thou shalt rejoice before the Lord thy God, thou, and thy son, and thy daughter, and thy man-servant, and thy maidservant, and the Levite that is within thy gates, and the stranger, and the fatherless, and the widow, that are in the midst of thee, in the place which the Lord thy God shall choose to cause His name to dwell there." [2]

2 Deut. xvi. 10-11.

The nature and amount of the freewill offering is here left to the liberality of the giver; and this seems to be the only one of the feasts held at the metropolis to which the stranger, fatherless, and widow are expressly named as persons to be invited. But the law contemplated other offerings also, the bringing of which was not obligatory, but which God expressed His willingness to accept from any of His

people who were disposed with a willing heart to give.
A famous example of this occurred at Sinai, at
the making of the tabernacle, when the Lord spoke
unto Moses, saying, "Speak unto the children of
Israel, that they take for Me an offering: of every
man whose heart maketh him willing, ye shall take
my offering,"[1] the result of this appeal being that
the people had to be restrained from bringing, "for
the stuff they had was sufficient for all the work
to make it, and too much."[2]

[1] Exod. xxv. 1.

[2] Exod. xxxvi. 7.

We have frequent mention also, in the law, of
vows and freewill offerings. It was directed that
"whosoever offereth a sacrifice of peace offerings
unto the Lord to accomplish a vow, or for a freewill
offering, of the herd or of the flock, it shall be
perfect to be accepted."[3] An imperfect bullock
or lamb might be brought for a freewill offering,
but not for a vow.[4] Other directions concerning
vows and devoted things take up nearly the whole
of the last chapter of Leviticus.

[3] Lev. xxii. 21.

[4] ver. 23.

The general rule, seemingly, for voluntary giving
at the festivals was this:

"Three times in a year shall all thy males appear before
the Lord thy God in the place which He shall choose;
in the feast of unleavened bread, and in the feast of weeks,
and in the feast of tabernacles: and they shall not appear
before the Lord empty: every man shall give as he is able,
according to the blessing of the Lord thy God which He
hath given thee."[5]

[5] Deut. xvi. 16-17.

At the same time, concerning vows generally, the
law enjoined:

"When thou shalt vow a vow unto the Lord thy God,
thou shalt not be slack to pay it: for the Lord thy God

will surely require it of thee: and it would be sin in thee. But if thou shalt forbear to vow, it shall be no sin in thee. That which is gone out of thy lips thou shalt observe and do; according as thou hast vowed unto the Lord thy God, a freewill offering, which thou hast promised with thy mouth." [1]

1 Deut. xxiii. 21-3.

Another general rule, that might be practised every day and everywhere, was:

" If there be with thee a poor man, one of thy brethren, within any of thy gates in thy land which the Lord thy God giveth thee, thou shalt not harden thine heart, nor shut thine hand from thy poor brother: but thou shalt surely open thine hand unto him, and shalt surely lend him sufficient for his need in that which he wanteth. . . . Thou shalt surely give him, and thine heart shall not be grieved when thou givest unto him: because that for this thing the Lord thy God shall bless thee in all thy work, and in all that thou puttest thine hand unto." [2]

2 Deut. xv. 7-8, 10.

Such, then, were the tithes and offerings of the Mosaic law. In some cases the amount or proportion due was definitely stated; in others it was not stated with precision—as, for instance, with the second and third tithes it is not stated whether each tithe was to be a tenth of the whole or a tenth of the remainder after the previous tithe or tithes had been deducted. Hence, to reduce to figures what an Israelite was called upon annually to pay, and encouraged to give, is not easy, especially in relation to such matters as the first-lings and tithes of cattle, and his own firstborn son, to say nothing of the fruit of young trees for four years, as well as debts not enforced in the seventh year.

If, however, we may suppose the case of a man

whose entire income for a year consisted of a standing crop of 6,000 ephahs of wheat, this total would be reduced, probably, by his tithes and offerings, somewhat as follows: .

Standing Crop of 6,000 Ephahs.

Tithing the remainder.	*Fixed Claims.*		Tithing the whole.
6,000 ÷ 60 — 100	Corners, gleanings, forgotten sheaves (Lev. xix. 9; Deut. xxiv. 19)	$\frac{1}{60}$	100
5,900 ÷ 40 —.150	Firstfruits (Deut. xxvi. 1-10) .	$\frac{1}{40}$	150
5,750 ÷ 10 — 575	The Lord's Tithe (Lev. xxvii. 30) .	$\frac{1}{10}$	600
5,175 ÷ 10 — 517	The Festival Tithe (Deut. xiv. 22) .	$\frac{1}{10}$	600
4,658 ÷ 30 — 155	The Poor's Tithe (Deut. xiv. 28) .	$\frac{1}{30}$	200
4,503 remainder.		To be deducted	1,650

Other Possible Deductions.

A freewill offering at the Feast of Weeks (Deut. xvi. 10).

Animals in payment of vows or things devoted (Lev. xxvii. 9, 28).

Remission of debts in year of release.

Redemption of firstborn.

Thankofferings generally.

From the foregoing it will be seen that if the standing crop amounts to 6,000 ephahs, or bushels, an estimated $\frac{1}{60}$ must be left in the corners, or as gleanings, or forgotten sheaves, for the poor. Then, of the remaining 5,900 bushels, an estimated

$\frac{1}{40}$ more is to be offered as firstfruits. From the 5,750 bushels left, the Lord's tithe for the Levites is to be taken, which reduces the ingathering to 5,175 bushels; and when from this the festival tithe is taken, it leaves to the owner 4,658 bushels. From this must be deducted $\frac{1}{30}$ (or a third of the triennial tithe), by which the net remainder is reduced to 4,503 bushels, or three-fourths of the original whole.

Out of this remainder, however, there might have to be provided the redemption for a firstborn son, or, once in seven years, the remission of debts; and from the same source, according to the owner's liberality, would come a freewill offering at the Feast of Weeks; and, on other occasions, animals for the payment of vows, or devoted things and thankofferings, generally.

So, then, on the principle of tithing the remainder, a liberal Israelite's outgoings would amount to, at least, a fourth of his income. On the other hand, if each item is charged upon the whole 6,000, then it will be seen that there would remain, after the payment of fixed claims, only 4,350. Added to this, the consumption of time for several weeks, for the observance of festivals, would be considerable; and if 350 bushels more may be regarded as an equivalent for this loss, as well as for redemption of the firstborn, remitted debts, for vows and freewill offerings, then a man's outgoings would amount, on this principle, to a third of his entire harvest.

Perhaps, therefore, we are justified in supposing

that the Mosaic law required the Israelite to set
apart, in some way or other connected with his
religion, from one-fourth to a third of his income.
Or, to put it in another away: a conscientious
man, wishful to act up to his duty, might begin by
setting apart a tenth of his income for the Lord's
tithe.   He would regard his firstborn and the firstlings of his cattle as belonging to the Lord.   The
fruit of young trees for three years he would not
eat, and on the fourth year would set apart the
fruit for God, whilst every seventh year he would
not claim money from his debtors.   At the time
of every harvest he would leave for the poor the
corners of his field, the gleanings and forgotten
sheaves, as well as fallen fruit and overlooked
olives and grapes.   He would then set aside a
second tenth for expenses connected with going
up to the sanctuary, taking with him a freewill
offering at the Feast of Weeks, and possibly animals
for payment of vows, or thankofferings, or things
devoted, in addition to his firstfruits.   These firstfruits he would put in a basket, and, coming to
the priest, would say to him : " I profess this day
unto the Lord thy God, that I am come unto the
land which the Lord sware unto our fathers for
to give us." [1]   [1] Deut. xxvi. 3.

Upon this the priest would take the basket and
set it down before the altar, and the offerer then
would solemnly say before God : [2]   [2] Deut. xxvi. 5.

" A Syrian ready to perish was my father, and he went
down into Egypt, and sojourned there, few in number ;
and he became there a nation, great, mighty, and populous :

and the Egyptians evil entreated us, and afflicted us, and laid upon us hard bondage: and we cried unto the Lord, the God of our fathers, and the Lord heard our voice, and saw our affliction, and our toil, and our oppression: and the Lord brought us forth out of Egypt with a mighty hand, and with an outstretched arm, and with great terribleness, and with signs, and with wonders: and He hath brought us into this place, and hath given us this land, a land flowing with milk and honey. And now, behold, I have brought the first of the fruit of the ground, which Thou, O Lord, hast given me."

The firstfruits thus dedicated, the offerer would worship before Jehovah, in gratitude and acknowledgment of all the good given to him, his family, the Levite, and the stranger.[1]

1 Deut. xxvi. 2-11.

This beautiful form was provided for yearly use, whilst every third year, a third tenth having been set apart for the local poor, our pious Israelite would solemnly declare before God:

" I have put away the hallowed things out of mine house, and also have given them unto the Levite, and unto the stranger, to the fatherless, and to the widow, according to all Thy commandment which Thou hast commanded me : I have not transgressed any of Thy commandments, neither have I forgotten them : I have not eaten thereof in my mourning, neither have I put away thereof, being unclean, nor given thereof for the dead : I have hearkened to the voice of the Lord my God, I have done according to all that Thou hast commanded me. Look down from Thy holy habitation, from heaven, and bless Thy people Israel, and the ground which Thou hast given us, as Thou swarest unto our fathers, a land flowing with milk and honey."[2]

2 Deut. xxvi. 13-15.

Having now collected various pieces of information concerning Mosaic tithes and offerings, we

do well to notice the nature of the evidence thus
brought together. Professor Driver, in his commentary on Deuteronomy,[1] would have us to believe [1 p. 172.]
that "the data at our disposal do not enable us to
write a history of the Hebrew tithe." But this is
no sufficient reason why we should not make the
most of the information we have, remembering,
however, that the evidence is not primary, direct,
and complete, so much as subsidiary, indirect, and
fragmentary.

We have not, for instance, throughout the
Pentateuch so much as a single chapter, or even
a long paragraph, dealing with tithe as a whole.
We have had to collect our information mainly
from three short passages in Leviticus, Numbers,
and Deuteronomy, these passages being there
introduced not so much for their own sakes as
for their bearing upon other things.

Thus the first authoritative statement (in the
generally received order of the books) of the great
foundation principle that a tenth of the produce of
the land and of beasts belongs to Jehovah, is not
ushered in, as we might expect, with the solemn
preamble, " The Lord said unto Moses, Speak unto
the children of Israel," etc. ; but we see this great
truth specifically mentioned for the first time at the
end of Leviticus, in a supplementary chapter regulating the making of vows and determining how far
things or animals devoted to God might be redeemed. Here the subject of the tithe comes in,
quite incidentally and without explanation ; and
then it is spoken of, not for the purpose of

enjoining it as something new, or as though it were not already in use, but in order to exclude the tithe portion from vows, and to prescribe how far and under what conditions, like vows, tithe might be redeemed.[1]

1 Lange's Commentary on Lev. xxvii. 30-3.

So again, in Numbers xviii., after the rebellion of Korah, when several laws are being given concerning the priests and Levites, this first tithe is again introduced, not so much, seemingly, for its own sake, as to show how the Levites, though having no inheritance among the tribes, are to be repaid for their labour by its appropriation to their benefit.

Once more, when we come to Deuteronomy xiv. we have a chapter regulating what may be eaten and what may not be eaten, of beasts, fishes, and fowls; and then follow directions concerning eating before God of the second tithe at an appointed place of worship.

Furthermore, what we are told about tithes is not only fragmentary, but it is also incomplete. The Mosaic law, for instance, does not define particularly what seeds, fruits, or animals are to be tithed; nor does the legislator give directions "whether the tenth is to be paid of all newly born animals; whether it includes those newly purchased or exchanged; whether it is payable if a man have less than ten cattle, or at what age of the animals the tithe becomes due."[2]

2 McClintock and Strong, x. p. 434.

Nor, as already observed, does the law say whether each tithe is to be computed in reference to the whole, or out of what remains after previous tithes have been deducted; nor, again, is it clear whether the second tithe includes a second tenth of all animals.*

The law concerning tithe, then, in general has in one respect a close resemblance to the law concerning the Sabbath. When Jehovah promulgated the Decalogue as a statute or written law, He said, "*Remember* the Sabbath to keep it holy," thereby implying that the commandment was already in existence or had been enjoined before; and the same might be said of other commandments which were laws of God and rules of life for man, and for keeping of which Abraham is praised, and for the non-observance of which punishment is recorded, long before Jehovah's laws were published on Sinai.[1] 1 See p. 20.

So, with regard to Mosaic tithes and offerings, it has been shown elsewhere that before the descendants of Jacob left Palestine it was a well-established custom in Egypt to make regular offerings to the gods and to pay to the temples firstfruits of the harvest,[2] so that with these customs, at any rate, the Israelites, on leaving Egypt, would be familiar. They would likewise remember that two-tenths,

2 See Sacred Tenth, p. 3.

* By way of illustration we may observe, as a somewhat parallel case, the importation of the word "fasting" into the Book of Common Prayer. In the prefatory matter is "A Table of the Fasts and Days of Abstinence," also a list of the days of fasting; and in the Communion Service the curate is directed to declare what fasting days are to be observed. But nothing is said as to *who* is to fast, nor in *what* fasting consists, *where* it should be observed, or with what *accessories*, nor *why* or *how*, but only *when*. Just, then, as these minutiæ, when the first English Prayer Book was issued, were well known and understood, and were taken so to be; so, presumably, the less needed to be said by the writer of the Pentateuch about the particulars connected with tithing, because the people were familiar with the custom as descended from their forefathers.

4

or a double tithe, of increase was paid by the
Egyptians to Pharaoh, who supported the priests,
and that, by virtue of the legislation of their own
ancestor, Joseph, whose bones they were taking
up for burial in the land of Canaan at the very
time their own law was given; whilst as for tithes,
how could the Israelites forget the observance of
this custom by their great ancestor Abraham, or
fail to remember the vow of his grandson Israel,
" Of all that thou shalt give me, I will surely give
the tenth unto Thee " ? [1]

1 Gen. xxviii. 22.

These things, presumably, must have been to
them as household words, and hence there can be
little doubt that the inspired legislator adopted the
already existing practice of tithe-paying, and inserted
it in the statute law of the divine code, because
he found that, with some modification, this ancient
payment might be made a proper stipend for the
servants and officers of the theocracy, and also that
second and third tithes might furnish the means of
promoting regular worship at the national sanctuary,
and foster social intercourse and good feeling between
rich and poor.*

We have thus reached, as already intimated, a
higher platform than any upon which we have yet
stood. We have emerged from the clouds of probability and conjecture concerning the origin of
tithe-paying, to see the custom recognized, regulated,
and embodied in what has been generally accepted
as a most ancient code of written laws.

It is claimed for this code that it was written by

* See McClintock and Strong's *Encyclopædia*, x. p. 436.

inspiration of the God of Israel, of whom Jews and Christians alike believe that He never yet made a law that was unjust or unwise, or that did not tend to His people's happiness. If, then, God has given laws upon tithe-paying, they are sure to be worthy of at least our respectful study, and we accordingly proceed to examine, so far as our data enable us, the working of these laws among the Israelites, from their entrance into Canaan down to the close of Old Testament history.

CHAPTER V

FROM JOSHUA TO SOLOMON

HAVING studied the laws of the Pentateuch
concerning tithes and offerings, we proceed
to inquire what further light may be obtained upon
tithe-paying from the working of these laws during
the period covered by the rest of the Old Testament,
taking the books in the generally received order.
This period may be conveniently divided into four
parts, beginning with the settlement of Canaan
under Joshua and the Judges, and taking next the
monarchy under Saul, David, and Solomon. A
third era begins with the divided kingdoms of
Judah and Israel, which may be followed by the
re-settlement of the land after the Babylonian
captivity.

As in previous chapters, let us search diligently
for passages concerning firstfruits, presents, and

dues to priests; for sacrifices, and instances of the offering of material things to God; as well as for examples of private beneficence in general, so that, in the absence of actual mention of tithes, we may see what can be inferred respecting them, as also concerning religious giving, and non-prescribed benevolence generally.

After crossing the Jordan, Joshua at once put in force the laws concerning circumcision and the observance of the Passover.[1]   Also, on coming to Mount Ebal, he built an altar unto Jehovah, offered burnt offerings, sacrificed peace offerings,[2] and wrote on the stones, in the presence of the people, a copy of the law of Moses. . . . "There was not a word of all that Moses commanded, which Joshua read not before all the congregation of Israel, with the women and the little ones, and the strangers that were conversant among them."[3]

[1] Josh. v.

[2] Josh. viii. 30-2.

[3] Josh. viii. 35.

Joshua read therefore all that was commanded about tithes; and, seeing that the only means of support of many thousands of Levites with their families was dependent on these contributions, we cannot suppose that this item of the law was permitted to remain a dead letter.   Nor, indeed, were the Levites slow to claim their rights, for they came to Joshua at Shiloh, saying: "The Lord commanded by the hand of Moses to give us cities to dwell in, with the suburbs thereof for our cattle";[4] and if they thus put in their claim for places to dwell in, which was allowed to the extent of forty-eight cities, it is not likely they would have

[4] Josh. xxi. 1-2; 1 Chron. vi. 57, etc.

failed, had there been need, to ask for their tithes also.

As for other kinds of offerings, when Joshua was directed to divide the land, it is expressly mentioned that "only unto the tribe of Levi he gave none inheritance; the offerings of the Lord, the God *1 Josh. xiii. 7-14.* of Israel, made by fire are his inheritance." [1]

Under the Judges we have an unsettled time, both politically and religiously. "There was no king in Israel; every man did that which was right *2 Judg. xvii. 6.* in his own eyes." [2] The priesthood no doubt suffered in common with others from this lawlessness, as indicated, perhaps, by the young Levite departing from Bethlehem-Judah to sojourn where he could find a place, and on coming to Mount Ephraim, to the house of Micah, was content to remain there for food, clothing, and shelter, coupled with the annual pittance of ten shekels *3 Judg. xvii. 8, etc.* of silver. [3]

Again, the foul treatment, at Gibeah, of a Levite and his concubine shows the men of Benjamin to have sunk at this period to a very degraded condition. Nevertheless, we observe indications both here and throughout the book of Judges, that the worship of Jehovah was still maintained; for when an angel came up from Gilgal to Bochim, and reproved the Israelites for not throwing down the altars of the inhabitants of the land, we read *4 Judg. ii. 2-5.* that the people wept and sacrificed to Jehovah. [4]

Also, when, under the oppression of the Midianites, some of the people fell away to Amorite gods, we find Gideon building an altar, calling it Jehovah-

Shalom, and offering thereon the bullock of the altar of Baal.[1]

1 Judg. vi. 10, 28.

Next we have Jephthah delivering Israel, after making a vow to his God that whatever might come forth out of the doors of his house to meet him on his return from victory, should be devoted to Jehovah, and offered as a burnt offering.[2]

2 Judg. xi. 31.

So, too, when Israel was oppressed by the Philistines, and Samson was to be raised up from the house of Manoah, it was to Jehovah that Manoah presented his burnt offering;[3] just as when Samson, having fallen into the enemy's hands, the lords of the Philistines gathered to offer a great sacrifice, and to rejoice before their god Dagon.[4]

3 Judg. xiii. 16.

4 Judg. xvi. 23.

Further, when Israel was collected from Dan even to Beersheba to punish the Benjamites for their wrongdoing at Gibeah, to the Levite and his concubine, the people gathered as one man before Jehovah in Mizpeh; the tribes presented themselves, we read, in the assembly of the people of God.[5] And when the punitive force sent against Gibeah was twice repulsed, the people came to the house of God, wept, fasted, offered burnt offerings and peace offerings, and inquired of Jehovah before the Ark of the Covenant, by Phinehas, grandson of Aaron, who stood before it in those days.[6]

5 Judg. xx. 1-2.

6 Judg. xx. 26-7.

Once more, when Gibeah had fallen, and wives were lacking to the surviving Benjamites, the people rose early, came to the house of God, and offered burnt offerings and peace offerings, whilst the closing scene of the book of Judges shows us, that, even at that time, there was held in Shiloh a yearly feast to Jehovah.

When we come to the days of Eli, religious affairs seem to be more settled. Shiloh is still the appointed place of worship whither Elkanah and all his house went up yearly to offer his sacrifice and his vow.[1] We learn, too, that it had become the priests' custom with the people, that when any man offered sacrifice, the priest's servant came, while the flesh was boiling, with a flesh-hook of three teeth in his hand, and he struck it into the pan, or kettle, or cauldron, or pot; all that the flesh-hook brought up the priest took for himself.[2]

This was done to all the Israelites who came to Shiloh; and since Eli and his sons were reproached for "making themselves fat" with the chiefest of all the offerings of Israel, it would seem to hint that the number of offerings and the multitude of people attending the feasts were large.

Under Samuel the Ark was for some months in possession of the Philistines, who sent it to Beth-shemesh with a trespass offering of golden tumours and mice, giving glory to the God of Israel.[3] At Beth-shemesh the Ark was taken from the cart by the Levites, and the wood of the cart, and the oxen that drew it, were offered as a burnt sacrifice, besides which the people of Beth-shemesh offered on that day burnt offerings and sacrifices.[4] The Ark was then taken to Kirjath-jearim, where Eleazar, the son of Abinadab, was appointed to keep it, and where it remained for twenty years, the people meanwhile falling away to the worship

1 1 Sam. i. 21.

2 1 Sam. ii. 13-14.

3 1 Sam. vi. 4-5.

4 1 Sam. vi. 15.

of Baalim and Ashtaroth, but at the same time lamenting after Jehovah.[1]

Accordingly Samuel gathered all Israel to Mizpeh, took a sucking-lamb, and offered it for a whole burnt offering, and cried unto the Lord for Israel, after which Samuel returned to Ramah, where was his house, and where he built an altar unto the Lord.[2]

Whilst, therefore, the period from Joshua to Samuel was one of religious unrest, of oppression by foreigners, and occasional and partial defection to strange gods, we see sufficient indications to show that the Ark was set up, that the worship of Jehovah was retained as the established religion of the people, and in accordance with this we may conclude that the claims of the Levites were more or less recognized and the tithes paid.

We come next to the period of the Israelitish monarchy, beginning with Saul, who is introduced to us whilst seeking his father's asses, and who is advised to ask direction of Samuel. Saul recognizes the standing custom that an offering must be made to the man of God,[3] to which end his servant proposes to give a quarter of a shekel of silver; and there happened to be a sacrifice that day on the high place to which Samuel had been invited.[4]

Soon after, at Gilgal, they made Saul king before the Lord, and sacrificed peace offerings, rejoicing before the Lord.[5]

But we do not learn much concerning divine offerings from the annals of this unsatisfactory

[1] 1 Sam. vii. 2-3.

[2] 1 Sam. vii. 9-17.

[3] 1 Sam. ix. 7.

[4] 1 Sam. ix. 12.

[5] 1 Sam. xi. 15.

monarch, though it is stated that some at least of his spoils won in battle he dedicated to repair the house of the Lord.   Samuel had so done before, as afterwards did Abner and Joab, the generals of Saul and David.[1]

1 1 Chron. xxvi. 27-8.

This bears upon our subject to some extent, because these Israelitish warriors at this early date were only doing as did their forefather Abram. They were carrying out a custom that extended far beyond the confines of Palestine, for we have now reached the supposed era of the Trojan war, when the Argives, as we are told, having subdued the Mycenians, are said to have consecrated a tenth of their goods to their god.[2]   The Philistines also, it may be remarked, were actuated apparently by similar motives on the downfall of Saul, by stripping his body and putting his armour in the house of the Ashtaroth.[3]

2 See Sacred Tenth, p. 22.

3 1 Sam. xxxi. 10.

In David, we have a monarch who was anointed king at a religious sacrifice or feast,[4] and the excuse which Jonathan made one day to account for David's absence from Saul's table, suggests that in Jesse's household, as with Elkanah's, there was a yearly sacrifice for all the family.[5]

4 1 Sam. xvi. 5.

5 1 Sam. xx. 6-29.

Moreover, David's first trophy taken in war—the sword of Goliath—we hear of subsequently as wrapped in a cloth behind the ephod, under the care of Ahimelech the priest;[6] whilst towards the end of David's reign, so great had become the number of spoils taken in war, that they were placed under the charge of Shelomith and his brethren, to whose care also were entrusted all the treasures of

6 1 Sam. xxi. 9.

the dedicated things which David, the chief fathers, and captains of the host, had dedicated out of the spoils taken in battles.[1]

On becoming king over all Israel, David lost no time in bringing the Ark of God to Jerusalem. When those that bare it had marched six paces, the king sacrificed oxen and fatlings.[2] The Levites also, on being helped by God, offered seven bullocks and seven rams ; and when the Ark was brought into the tent prepared for it, David further offered burnt sacrifices and peace offerings before God,[3] after which he blessed the people in the name of Jehovah, and dealt to every man and woman a loaf of bread, a portion of flesh, and a cake of raisins.[4]

After this, David appointed a large number of priests and Levites to perform daily service before the high place at Gibeon, to offer burnt offerings unto the Lord upon the altar of the burnt offering continually morning and evening, and to do according to all that is written in the law of the Lord.[5]

Then David consulted Nathan about building a temple, for which the king began to collect materials, dedicating thereto the silver and the gold that he took from all the nations: from Edom, from Moab, and from the children of Ammon, and from the Philistines, from Amalek, and the spoil of Hadadezer,[6] which strongly reminds us of the way in which the Egyptian and Babylonian kings dedicated their spoils to their gods.

Later on we see the royal penitent purchasing the

[1] 1 Chron. xxvi. 26-7.

[2] 2 Sam. vi. 13.

[3] 1 Chron. xv. 26, xvi. 1-2.

[4] 1 Chron. xvi. 3.

[5] 1 Chron. xvi. 37-40.

[6] 1 Chron. xviii. 11; 2 Sam. viii. 11-12.

threshing-floor of Ornan the Jebusite for six
hundred shekels of gold, because he would not
offer burnt offerings without cost ; and building
thereon an altar because he was afraid to go before
the tabernacle in the high place at Gibeon.[1]

[1] 1 Chron. xxi.
24-5, 29.

Then began David's active preparation of materials
for the temple, comprising three thousand talents
of gold, seven thousand talents of silver, also brass,
iron, wood, marble, costly stones, and onyx and
other gems.[2] This example was followed by the
princes to the extent of five thousand talents, and
ten thousand drams, of gold, ten thousand talents
of silver, eighteen thousand talents of brass, one
hundred thousand talents of iron, as well as costly
stones ; the king and people rejoicing for that they
offered willingly.[3] After this they killed, as burnt
offerings, one thousand bullocks, one thousand rams,
one thousand lambs with their drink offerings, and
sacrifices for all Israel, who ate and drank before
the Lord with great gladness.[4]

[2] 1 Chron. xxix.
2-4.

[3] 1 Chron. xxix.
6-9.

[4] 1 Chron. xxix.
21-2

Moreover, David appointed the services for the
priests and Levites, the number of Levites above
thirty years of age alone being thirty-eight thousand
(which, with their families, would probably mean
nearly two hundred thousand persons[5]), in addition
to whom there were appointed several courses of
priests.[6]

[5] 1 Chron. xxiii.
3-5.

[6] 1 Chron. xxiv.

We now come to the days of Solomon, who, at
the beginning of his reign, offered one thousand
burnt offerings at Gibeon ;[7] and after his dream,
offered before the Ark at Jerusalem burnt and peace
offerings, and made a feast to all his servants.

[7] 1 Kings iii. 4;
2 Chron. i. 6.

When the time came for the dedication of the temple, the Ark was brought to its place, with sacrifices innumerable of sheep and oxen,[1] after which Solomon and the people offered to the Lord twenty-two thousand oxen and one hundred and twenty thousand sheep, holding a feast for all Israel during fourteen days.[2]

[1] 1 Kings viii. 5.

[2] 1 Kings viii. 63, 65; 2 Chron. v. 6, vii. 3-10.

After this we find Solomon, "after a certain rate every day offering, according to the commandment of Moses, on the sabbaths, and on the new moons, and on the solemn feasts, three times in the year."[3]

[3] 2 Chron. viii. 12-16; 1 Kings ix. 25.

We may now, therefore, consider the worship of Jehovah fully established and carried out according to the law of the Pentateuch. But from the entrance of the people into Canaan to the reign of Solomon—a space of nearly five hundred years— we have found nothing specifically mentioned about tithes. Samuel came very near to the word when, the Israelites having asked for a king, the prophet warned them " he will take the tenth of your seed, . . . he will take the tenth of your sheep, and ye shall be his servants." [4]

[4] 1 Sam. viii. 15-17.

Hence, certain writers have imagined that some of the kings took for themselves the Levites' tithes. But the scripture does not say so. Solomon indeed raised a levy out of all Israel of two hundred and sixteen thousand men who were foreigners and not of the children of Israel,[5] and if for the support of these two hundred and sixteen thousand work-men an extra tenth were imposed, in addition to the Mosaic tenths that would undoubtedly be claimed by the two hundred thousand Levitical

[5] 1 Kings v. 13-16; 2 Chron. ii. 2, 17, viii. 9.

persons, we can understand the people coming to Solomon's son and saying, " Thy father made our yoke grievous." [1]

But we never read that the payment of Mosaic tithes and offerings was an undue burden. On the contrary, and speaking generally, we may say that the more closely God's law was kept the more prosperous were the people.

1 1 Kings xii. 4.

CHAPTER VI

BEFORE AND AFTER THE CAPTIVITY

Working of tithe-laws during two further periods: III. Under Judah and Israel, 63.—Reformations under Asa and Jehoshaphat, 64. —Giving in the times of Elijah and Elisha, 64.—Church repairs under Joash, 66.—Amos on Israel's tithes, 67.—Hezekiah's restoration of Passover, tithe-paying, and firstfruits, 68.—Temple repairs and offerings under Josiah, 70.—IV. After the Captivity, 71.—Offerings from Cyrus, 71.—Rebuilding and presents to Temple under Ezra, 72.—Malachi's "robbery" for withholding tithes, 73.—Nehemiah's offering, and the people's oath concerning tithes, 73.—Tithing organized, 74.—Review of tithing from Joshua to Malachi, 75.

W E have now reached the high-water mark of religious giving in the Old Testament; and our next period, under the rival kings of Judah and Israel, is a period of declension, though retarded from time to time by temporary endeavours at reformation.

The schismatical Jeroboam found it politic to imitate the law of Moses in ordaining a feast like that held in Judah, and in sacrificing and placing priests at Bethel.[1] When, however, his own son was ill, he sent to inquire of the prophet Ahijah, at Shiloh, by his wife, who, in disguise, took as a present ten loaves, and cracknels, and a cruse of honey[2]: a suitable religious offering, presumably,

[1] 1 Kings xii. 32.

[2] 1 Kings xiv. 3.

at that time for a well-to-do woman of the country.

A little later, in Asa, king of Judah, we have a godly man, to whom is vouchsafed victory over the Ethiopians, and thereby much spoil:

"And they sacrified unto the Lord in that day, of the spoil which they had brought, 700 oxen and 7,000 sheep. . . . And Asa brought into the house of God the things that his father had dedicated, and that he himself had dedicated, silver, and gold, and vessels." [1]

1 2 Chron. xiv. 13, xv. 11-18; 1 Kings xv. 15.

This, however, was of the nature of a reformation; for Azariah, the son of Oded, reminded Asa that for a long season Israel had been without the true God, and without a teaching priest, and without law. [2] Furthermore, a similar work of reformation was carried on by Jehoshaphat his successor, who sent out teaching princes, Levites, and priests. "And they taught in Judah, having the book of the law of the Lord with them," so that "the fear of Jehovah fell upon all the kingdoms of the lands that were round about Judah." [3]

2 2 Chron. xv. 3.

3 2 Chron. xvii. 7-10.

This brings us to the days of Elijah and Elisha, in connection with whom we have several instances of pious beneficence in private life. Foremost among them is the widow of Zarephath, who had but a handful of meal in a barrel and a little oil in a cruse, but who, nevertheless, made thereof, first, a cake for the Lord's prophet. [4]

4 1 Kings xvii. 12-15.

Then follows the case of the godly Obadiah, who, although connected with Ahab's heathenish court, yet feared Jehovah greatly, and took a hundred prophets, persecuted by Jezebel, and hid

them by fifty in a cave, and fed them with bread
and water.[1] We also read in the same chapter of [1] 1 Kings xviii. 4.
the sacrifice of bullocks to Baal and to Jehovah,
respectively, on Mount Carmel.[2]   [2] 1 Kings xviii.

As for Elisha, we remember the kind hospitality
afforded him, as a man of God, by the woman of
Shunem, who prepared for him a little chamber on
the wall.[3] It seems also to have been customary [3] 2 Kings iv. 8-10.
for the people to bring offerings to Elisha: for
"there came a man from Baal-shalishah, and
brought the man of God bread of the firstfruits,
twenty loaves of barley, and fresh ears of corn,"
with which Elisha furnished a meal for the
people.[4]   [4] 2 Kings iv. 42.

The present which Naaman brought to Elisha
was evidently intended to be a valuable one, con-
sisting, as it did, of robes and talents of silver—
a typical acknowledgment of expected help from
the prophet in the cure of leprosy.[5] Benhadad [5] 2 Kings v.
also, when sending Hazael to inquire whether his 22-3.
master would recover of his sickness, sent forty
camel-loads of every good thing of Damascus.[6] [6] 2 Kings viii.
                                                     8-9.

The last-mentioned two instances of religious
offering are by Gentiles from outside the land of
Israel. Another instance of religious dedication is
that of Mesha, king of Moab, who, in a beleaguered
city, took his eldest son and offered him for a
burnt offering upon the wall.[7] Again, the prophet [7] 2 Kings iii. 27.
Jonah is thought to have lived about this time;
and if so, the proposal to offer to the gods their
passenger as a sacrifice, by casting him overboard,
would not be an abnormal or strange notion to

5

Jonah's shipmates. Moreover, observing that after so doing the sea became calm, they deemed their prayer answered, feared Jehovah exceedingly, offered a sacrifice, and made vows.[1]

1 Jonah i. 15-16.

This mixing up of true and false religious worship and offerings is further illustrated by Jehu, who proclaimed that he had a great sacrifice to do to Baal, and then put to death Baal's priests.[2]

2 2 Kings x. 19-25.

We now come to the days of the youthful Joash, who did right so long as he was directed by Jehoiada the priest. Even the wicked Athaliah, who had broken up the house of God, bestowed the dedicated things upon the Baalim.[3] Joash accordingly proposed to the priests that all the money of the dedicated things brought into the house of the Lord, and all voluntary gifts, should be taken for temple repairs. But the priests did not forward the matter: whereupon Joash asked why the repairs were not done; after which the priests consented to receive no more money of the people; but neither did they consent to make good the repairs.[4]

3 2 Chron. xxiv. 2-7.

4 2 Kings xii. 4-8.

The king, however, being minded to restore the house of the Lord, gathered the priests and Levites, and said to them: " Go out unto the cities of Judah, and gather of all Israel money to repair the house of your God from year to year." But the Levites did not bestir themselves.[5]

5 2 Chron. xxiv. 5.

Then the king commanded, and they made a chest, bored a hole in the lid, and set it beside the altar; and the priests that kept the door put therein all the money that was brought into the house.

This money was given to the workmen for repairs, but not expended for making sacred vessels. Also the trespass-money and sin-money were not brought into the house of the Lord: it was the priests'.[1] [1] 2 Kings xii. 9-16. We read again of this chest, or one like it, set without, at the gate of the house of the Lord,[2] con- [2] 2 Chron. xxiv. 8. cerning which they made a proclamation, throughout Judah and Jerusalem, to bring in for the Lord the tax (presumably the half shekel[3]) that Moses the [3] Exod. xxx. 13. servant of God laid upon Israel in the wilderness. Thus they gathered money in abundance. The workmen wrought, and when they had finished the house, they made of the rest of the money vessels for the temple, after which, we read, they offered burnt offerings in the house of the Lord continually all the days of Jehoiada.[4] [4] 2 Chron. xxiv. 4-14.

But after the death of Jehoiada, Joash forsook the house of Jehovah, and, with the princes, fell away to idols, so that wrath came upon Judah and Jerusalem for their guiltiness.[5] [5] 2 Chron. xxiv. 17-18.

Nor do things appear to have been any better at this time in Israel, if we may judge from the ironical and derisive words of Amos, who prophesied some few years later:

"Come to Bethel and transgress; to Gilgal and multiply transgression; and bring your sacrifices every morning, and your tithes every three days; and offer a sacrifice of thanksgiving of that which is leavened, and proclaim free-will offerings, and publish them; for this liketh you, O ye children of Israel."[6] [6] Amos iv. 5.

These sarcastic words seem to bid the people go on in their rebellion, reminding them, however, that they were already suffering punishment. " I also have given you cleanness of teeth in all your cities, and want of bread in all your places ; yet have ye not returned unto Me, saith the Lord." [1]

1 Amos iv. 6.

This is the first time we have met with the word "tithes" since its occurrence in the Pentateuch ; but tithes are now mentioned in such a way as to suggest that they were normally paid by Israel, only, in this case, for the worship of the golden calves. This condition of things, so far as Israel was concerned, was brought to a close by the carrying away of the ten tribes to Babylon, about B.C. 721.

As for the kingdom of Judah, the established religion had been almost annihilated under Ahaz, who sacrificed to the gods of Damascus, introduced strange worship into the temple, and then shut up the doors of the house of the Lord.[2]

2 2 Chron. xxviii. 22-4; 2 Kings xvi. 12.

This was the condition of things when Hezekiah came to the throne, and that monarch in the first year of his reign re-opened the doors of the house of the Lord.[3] Incense and burnt offering had ceased, and the vessels of the house of the Lord had been cast away under Ahaz.[4] All this was at once changed by Hezekiah, who offered seven bullocks, seven rams, seven lambs, and seven he-goats for a sin offering ; the Levites and priests were restored in the order prescribed by David ; and the congregation offered 70 bullocks, 100 rams, and 200 lambs as burnt offerings. Also among the consecrated things were 600 oxen and 3,000 sheep ; and the house of God was set in order.[5] After this

3 2 Chron. xxix. 3.

4 2 Chron. xxix. 7-19.

5 2 Chron. xxix. 21, 32-5.

Hezekiah observed the Passover tor fourteen days, giving for offerings 1,000 bullocks and 7,000 sheep; whilst the princes added 1,000 bullocks and 10,000 sheep.[1]

1 2 Chron. xxx. 24.

Now, when the priests and Levites were thus re-appointed, the king's portion of his substance for burnt offerings was arranged for the services according to the law; and Hezekiah commanded the people in Jerusalem to furnish the portion of the priests and Levites, that they might give themselves to the law of the Lord; whereupon, as soon as the commandment was promulgated, the children of Israel gave in abundance the firstfruits of corn, wine, oil, and honey, and the tithe of all things brought they in abundantly; whilst the people living in the towns of Judah brought in the tithe of oxen and sheep, and the tithe of dedicated things, and laid them by heaps.[2]

2 2 Chron. xxxi. 3-6.

Questioned concerning these heaps, the chief priest said, "Since the people began to bring the oblations into the house of the Lord, we have eaten and had enough, and have left plenty; for the Lord hath blessed His people; and that which is left is this great store." Then Hezekiah prepared chambers in the house of the 'Lord, and the people brought faithfully oblations, tithes, and dedicated things, over which two Levites were appointed chief rulers, with ten overseers under them.[3] Besides this, another Levite was over the freewill offerings, and under him were six assistants to distribute the oblations of the Lord to the Levites in their courses, and to the priests in their cities; and in every town

3 2 Chron. xxxi. 10-13.

men were appointed to give portions to the priests, and to all that were reckoned by genealogy among the Levites, their little ones, wives, sons, and daughters.[1]

1 2 Chron. xxxi. 14-19.

From this reformation by Hezekiah we may reasonably deduce that the closing of the temple had brought poverty upon the priests and Levites, but that, on the restoration of the services, the normal state of things was restored, and the payment anew of the tithes and offerings brought back peace and plenty.

The next king, Manasseh, re-established idolatry, and was taken captive to Babylon ; but, being restored to his kingdom in Jerusalem in answer to prayer, he took away the strange gods out of the temple, built up the altar of Jehovah, and offered thereon sacrifices.[2] On the other hand, Amon, his son, sacrificed to the graven images which Manasseh, his father, had made.[3]

2 2 Chron. xxxiii. 1-16.

3 2 Chron. xxxiii. 22.

We now come to Josiah, the last of the reforming kings of Judah, who, after purging the land of idolatry, directed the money collected by the Levites at the door of the temple, from all Judah, Benjamin, and Jerusalem, as well as from the peoples of Manasseh, Ephraim, and the remnant of all Israel, to be expended on temple repairs. In the course of these repairs a copy of the law of the Lord was discovered. The king at once gathered the elders of Judah and Jerusalem, and they made a covenant to perform the law, and all the people stood to the covenant.[4]

4 2 Kings xxiii. 1-3.

Then Josiah kept a Passover, and gave of his own

substance 3,000 bullocks and 30,000 sheep, lambs, and kids. Three rulers of the house of God gave to the priests, for Passover offerings, 2,600 small cattle and 300 oxen. Several chiefs of the Levites gave also to the Levites, for Passover offerings, 5,000 small cattle and 500 oxen, all being done as it is written in the law of Moses.[1]

[1] 2 Chron. xxxv. 1-9, 12.

" Notwithstanding, the Lord turned not from the fierceness of His great wrath": but said, " I will remove Judah also out of My sight," [2] which was done by their being taken captive to Babylon by Nebuchadnezzar, about 588 B.C. This closes the period of decline under the divided kingdoms of Judah and Israel.

[2] 2 Kings xxiii. 26-27.

We now pass to the re-settlement of Palestine by the captives returned from Babylon. During the period passed by the Jews in captivity they doubtless became lax in some of their religious observances; but about 536 B.C. Cyrus proclaimed that he was "charged" to build Jehovah a house at Jerusalem, and he offered facilities for the Jews to return.

Accordingly, when the chief of the fathers of Judah and Benjamin, and the priests and the Levites, prepared to leave, those remaining in Babylon "strengthened their hands with" gifts. Cyrus himself gave back the vessels which Nebuchadnezzar had taken from the temple, "all the vessels of gold and silver being 5,400";[3] so that when the offerings of the king, his counsellors, and his lords, and all Israel present, were weighed for the house of God at Jerusalem, the treasure amounted to "650 talents of silver, 100 talents of

[3] Ezra i. 6-11.

silver vessels, 100 talents of gold, 20 bowls of gold of 1,000 darics, and two vessels of fine copper precious as gold." [1]

On their arrival in Jerusalem, "some of the chiefs of the fathers . . . offered freely for the house of God to set it up in his place. They gave after their ability . . . 61,000 darics of gold, 5,000 pound of silver, and 100 priests' robes." [2]   We read also of a subsequent burnt offering, by returned captives, of 12 bullocks for all Israel, 96 rams, 77 lambs, and 12 he-goats for a sin offering. [3]

When the seventh month was come, the people "gathered as one man to Jerusalem," built the altar of the God of Israel, and restored the continual daily burnt offering, and other customary offerings, as well for the feasts, as for "every one that willingly offered a freewill offering unto the Lord." [4]

The rebuilding of the temple having been stopped for some years, the work was again favoured by king Darius, who ordered that of the king's goods expenses should be given to the builders :

> "And that which they have need of, both young bullocks, and rams, and lambs, for burnt offerings to the God of heaven, wheat, salt, wine, and oil, according to the word of the priests which are at Jerusalem, let it be given them day by day without fail : that they may offer sacrifices of sweet savour unto the God of heaven, and pray for the life of the king, and of his sons." [5]

The house, accordingly, was finished, and the dedication kept with joy, the people offering at the dedication 100 bullocks, 200 rams, 400 lambs, and, for a sin offering, 12 he-goats ; after which, "they

1 Ezra viii. 26-7.

2 Ezra iii. 68-9.

3 Ezra viii. 35.

4 Ezra iii. 2-5.

5 Ezra vi. 8-10.

set the priests in their divisions, and the Levites in their courses, as it is written in the book of Moses." [1]

1 Ezra vi. 16-18.

So much, then, for information from the book of Ezra, which represents the worship of Jehovah restored, and the priests and Levites settled in their offices; but no mention is made as to how they were to be permanently supported. We read again of tithes, however, in the book of Nehemiah and in the prophecy of Malachi, who, by some, is thought to have been Nehemiah's contemporary and assistant in the work of reformation.

The prophet Malachi rebukes his contemporaries sharply for their defection from the law. He charges the priests with despising God's name in offering polluted bread upon the altar, and the blind, the lame, and the sick for sacrifice. [2]

2 Mal. i. 7-8; iv. 4.

Furthermore, in reference to tithes, the prophet's words are still more drastic; and he calls the people "robbers" for withholding them:

"Will a man rob God? yet ye rob Me. But ye say, Wherein have we robbed Thee? In tithes and offerings. Ye are cursed with the curse; for ye rob Me, even this whole nation. Bring ye the whole tithe into the storehouse, that there may be meat in Mine house, and prove Me now herewith, saith the Lord of hosts, if I will not open you the windows of heaven, and pour you out a blessing, that there shall not be room enough to receive it." [3]

3 Mal. iii. 8-10.

And almost the last words of Malachi are: "Remember ye the law of Moses my servant." [4]

4 Mal. iv. 4.

In view of these exhortations, it is satisfactory to observe that Nehemiah himself gave to the treasury 1,000 darics of gold, 50 basons, and 530 priests' robes. Heads of fathers' houses gave 20,000 darics of gold and 2,200 pound of silver; whilst the rest of the people gave 20,000 darics of gold, 2,000 pound of silver, and 67 priests' robes.[1]

1 Neh. vii. 70-2.

Later on we have that remarkable gathering when the children of Israel "assembled fasting, and with sackcloth and earth upon them," at the conclusion of which they "entered into a curse, and into an oath to walk in God's law, which was given by Moses the servant of God." The principal features of the oath were, not to marry heathens, nor purchase on the sabbath; to leave the land to rest in the seventh year, and not to enforce debts:

"Also . . . we made ordinances for us to charge ourselves yearly with the third part of a shekel for the service of the house of our God. . . . And we cast lots . . . for the wood offering . . . to burn upon the altar . . . and to bring the firstfruits of our ground, and the firstfruits of all fruit of all manner of trees, year by year, unto the house of the Lord; also the firstborn of our sons, and of our cattle . . . and the firstlings of our herds and of our flocks . . . and the firstfruits of our dough, and our heave offerings, and the fruit of all manner of trees, the vintage and the oil, unto the priests . . . and the tithes of our ground unto the Levites . . . and the Levites shall bring up the tithe of the tithes unto the house of our God . . . and we will not forsake the house of our God."[2]

2 Neh. x. 29-39.

Once more we read, that when the city wall was to be dedicated, the Levites were brought to Jerusalem, where they "offered great sacrifices, and rejoiced":

"And on that day were men appointed over the chambers for the treasures, for the heave offerings, for the firstfruits, and for the tithes, to gather into them, according to the fields of the cities, the portions appointed by the law for the priests and Levites: for Judah rejoiced for the priests and for the Levites that waited." [1]

1 Neh. xii. 27, 43-4.

How far, then, do these passages from the Old Testament illustrate the Mosaic law concerning tithes and offerings?

We may notice, in the first place, that, after the arrival of the Israelites in Canaan, the divine law was speedily put in force as a working institution. This included the rules for the devotion of tithes and offerings; and various intimations imply that the obligation of such tithes and offerings was actually and strictly recognized.

A central place of worship was established and sustained, whither the tribes went up to the feasts, in connection with which we read of priests and Levites by tens of thousands; or (if we add their families) by hundreds of thousands. These included not only those who waited about the altar, but the educational or teaching staff of the nation, as well as judicial officers, represented by judges and magistrates. [2]

2 1 Chron. xxiii. 4; Ezra viii. 25.

To these persons were given several cities and their suburbs wherein to live; but their appointed means of support was a tithe of the increase of the land and of cattle, with other offerings of the people. No other opportunity of obtaining a livelihood remained to them; for the tribe of Levi was not reckoned when the land was divided. Regard, therefore, for the maintenance of the law, such as we have seen exemplified from time to time by the whole nation, to say nothing of civil advantages brought to the people by the Levites, forbid us to think that the people, under ordinary circumstances, defrauded the Levites of the portion assigned them by God.

We may further observe that the law of Moses not only proved practicable, but, so far as tithes and religious offerings are concerned, we do not find it complained of as burdensome or oppressive—not even when, to pay Persian tribute, the people had mortgaged their lands.[1]

1 Neh. v. 3-4.

Nor do we read, during all the centuries in which tithe-paying was observed as a working institution, of any request being made that the tithe should be repealed or lessened. Even the heretical Jeroboam (if we rightly understand the words of Amos[2]) does not appear to have abolished the payment of tithes for religious purposes.

2 See p. 67.

Later on, when the people fell away to the worship of false gods, or were oppressed under a foreign yoke, we see how, in their times of humiliation, they took upon themselves afresh to observe the law of Moses, including tithes, always reverting to the Pentateuch as their standard of right living, but never questioning their obligation as to religious payments in general, or the proportion prescribed. It seems clear, indeed, that some of the people did not come up to the required standard during the reign of the wicked Ahaz, nor about the time of the return from captivity, when Malachi reproved such defaulters as " robbers of God." But these episodes seem to have been exceptions, and not the general rule.

Putting together, therefore, what we have thus far learned of our subject, we conclude that as secular history tells of other nations, such as the Babylonians, Carthaginians, Greeks, and Romans, dedicating a tenth of their income and spoils to their gods, so the people of Israel, from their settlement in Canaan to the end of the period covered by the Old Testament, did likewise ; the proportion payable by the Israelite, being a tenth applied to the use of the ministers of the sanctuary, and other tenths and offerings as prescribed by the law of the Pentateuch.

CHAPTER VII

TITHING IN THE APOCRYPHA

WE now proceed (in the next three chapters) to the study of tithe-paying and religious beneficence as taught and practised in Palestine during the period between the Old and New Testaments; taking as our sources of information the Apocrypha and the Talmud.

Whatever may be thought, theologically, of the doctrinal authority of the books of the Apocrypha, their antiquity and oriental authorship make them valuable as illustrating the ideas and customs of the period of which they are historical documents. Bearing this in mind, we proceed to search therein for passages concerning tithes, firstfruits, and religious offerings, as well as for examples of, and exhortations to, private beneficence generally. The books giving us most information on our subject are Tobit, Judith, Ecclesiasticus, and Maccabees.

The book of Tobit is especially useful in showing that it was thought right for a good man, as already observed,[1] to pay three tithes ; that is to say, an annual tenth for the Levites, a second tenth for the yearly festivals, and, triennially, a tenth for the poor.[2]

[1] See p. 32.

[2] Tobit i. 7-8.

Tobit himself is represented as a liberal giver. To Gabael, who had accompanied Tobias, the son of Tobit, to Nineveh, and faithfully brought him back with goods, servants, cattle, and money, both father and son thought it not too much to give a half of what had been brought, which represented ample wages and something more.[3] Also we read of Tobit that he did many almsdeeds to his brethren and his nation, for in the days of Shalmaneser he gave his bread to the hungry and his garments to the naked, and if he saw any of the race of Israel dead and cast forth on the wall of Nineveh, he buried him.[4]

[3] Tobit xii. 1-2.

[4] Tobit i. 3-16.

Passing now to the book of Judith, we find recorded an instance of the world-wide practice of vows and offerings made in prospect of war, followed by presentation of spoils after victory. Thus :

"Joakim the high priest . . . offered the continual burnt offering, and the vows and free gifts of the people : and they had ashes on their mitres, and they cried unto the Lord with all their power, that He would look upon the house of Israel for good."[5]

[5] Judith iv. 14. 15.

Further, when Judith had cut off the head of Holofernes, we read that the people offered their whole burnt offerings, freewill offerings, and their gifts, and that Judith dedicated all the stuff of Holofernes which the people had given her, and gave the canopy, which she had taken for herself, out of his bedchamber, for a gift unto the Lord.[1]

Some regard the books of Tobit and of Judith not as real histories, but as pious and instructive stories only. But even if this be so, the stories may be presumed to reflect the manners and customs of their age; and for our purpose they harmonize with the statements of the first book of the Maccabees, which is certainly, in the main, historical. Thus, on the cleansing of the Temple by Judas Maccabeus, we read they "offered sacrifice according to the law, upon the new altar of burnt offerings";[2] and in the same chapter it is related that among the promises made by Demetrius to secure the support of the Jews, one was that Ptolemais and its lands should be given to the Temple at Jerusalem, for the expenses that befit the sanctuary.[3]

Furthermore, in the second book of the Maccabees it is stated that the kings of the Gentiles glorified the Temple with the noblest presents, and that Seleucus, the king of Asia, of his own revenues bore all the costs belonging to the service of the sacrifices.[4]

Likewise, in the case of Heliodorus, chancellor of the governor of Cœlo-Syria, we have a Gentile officer who, being struck with a loathsome disease, was prayed for by Onias, the high-priest; whereupon, on recovery, Heliodorus offered a sacrifice unto Jehovah, and vowed great vows unto Him that had saved his life.[5]

1 Judith xvi. 18-19.

2 1 Macc. iv. 53.

3 1 Macc. iv. 39.

4 2 Macc. iii. 3.

5 2 Macc. iii. 35.

Again, king Seleucus, smitten on his way to Jerusalem by disease, vowed unto the Sovereign Lord, saying on this wise:

"That the holy city to which he was going in haste, to lay it even with the ground, and to make it a common graveyard, he would declare free: and, as touching the Jews whom he had decided not even to count worthy of burial, but to cast them out to the beasts, with their infants, for the birds to devour, he would make them all equal to citizens of Athens; and the holy sanctuary, which before he had spoiled, he would adorn with goodliest offerings, and would restore all the sacred vessels many times multiplied, and out of his own revenues would defray the charges that were required for the sacrifices; and, besides all this, that he would become a Jew, and would visit every inhabited place, publishing abroad the might of God." [1]

[1] 2 Macc. ix. 14. 17.

Yet another charitable action is attributed to Judas Maccabeus, who, on discovering that his Jewish followers had acted wrongly in touching dead bodies of idolaters, exhorted the multitude to keep themselves from sin. "And when he had made a collection, man by man, to the sum of two thousand drachmas of silver, he sent into Jerusalem to offer a sacrifice for sin, doing therein right well and honourably." [2]

[2] 2 Macc. xii. 38-43.

If now we pass from alleged facts, to principles, or exhortations concerning religious giving, we have Tobit saying: "Give of thy bread to the hungry, and of thy garments to them that are naked: of all thine abundance give alms." [3]

[3] Tobit iv. 16.

It is also clear that the author of the book of Tobit regarded the giving of alms as pleasing to God, and a means of obtaining the divine blessing.

6

He also thought that giving should be done with discrimination, and in proportion to a man's income. Exhorting his young son as to his manner of life, Tobit says:

"Give alms of thy substance; and when thou givest alms, let not thine eye be envious: turn not away thy face from any poor man, and the face of God shall not be turned away from thee. As thy substance is, give alms of it according to thine abundance: if thou have little, be not afraid to give alms according to that little; for thou layest up a good treasure for thyself against the day of necessity: because alms delivereth from death, and suffereth not to come into darkness. Alms is a good gift in the sight of the Most High for all that give it." [1]

1 Tobit iv. 7-11.

And to show that almsgiving should be performed with discrimination, he added: " Pour out thy bread on the burial of the just, and give nothing to sinners." [2]

2 Tobit iv. 16-17.

Later on in life Tobit advised his son Tobias thus:

" Good is prayer with fastings and alms, and righteousness. A little with righteousness is better than much with unrighteousness. It is better to give alms than to lay up gold: alms doth deliver from death, and it shall purge away all sin. They that do alms and righteousness shall be filled with life." [3]

3 Tobit xii. 8-10.

It is noteworthy also that the principles practised during early life, Tobit could recommend still in old age; for we read that on recovering his sight, at threescore and six, " he gave alms, and feared the Lord more and more," whilst the concluding words of his deathbed sayings were: " And now, my children, consider what alms doeth, and how righteousness doth deliver." [4]

4 Tobit xiv. 2-11.

These principles, taught in Tobit, are re-echoed and enlarged upon in *Ecclesiasticus, or the Wisdom of Jesus the Son of Sirach*, wherein we read, concerning gifts to God and His ministers, " My son, according as thou hast, do well unto thyself, and bring offerings unto the Lord worthily." [1]   More fully this same writer says :

[1] Ecclus. xiv. 11.

" He that keepeth the law multiplieth offerings ;
  He that taketh heed to the commandments sacrificeth a
    peace offering.
  He that requiteth a good turn offereth fine flour :
  And he that giveth alms sacrificeth a thank offering.
  To depart from wickedness is a thing pleasing to the Lord ;
  And to depart from unrighteousness is a propitiation.
  See that thou appear not in the presence of the Lord
    empty.
  For all these things are to be done because of the com-
    mandment.
  The offering of the righteous maketh the altar fat ;
  And the sweet savour thereof is before the Most High.
  The sacrifice of a righteous man is acceptable ;
  And the memorial thereof shall not be forgotten.
  Glorify the Lord with a good eye,
  And stint not the firstfruits of thine hands.
  In every gift show a cheerful countenance,
  And dedicate thy tithes with gladness.
  Give unto the Most High according as He hath given ;
  And as thy hand hath found, give with a good eye.
  For the Lord recompenseth,
  And He will recompense thee sevenfold." [2]

[2] Ecclus. xxxv. 1-11.

The following is much to the same effect :

" Fear the Lord with all thy soul ;
  And reverence His priests.
  With all thy strength love Him that made thee :
  And forsake not His ministers.

Fear the Lord and glorify the priest:
And give him his portion, even as it is commanded thee:
The firstfruits, and the trespass offering, and the gift of
　the shoulders,
And the sacrifice of sanctification, and the firstfruits of
　holy things.
Also to the poor man stretch out thy hand,
That thy blessing may be perfected." [1]

1 Ecclus. vii. 29-32.

This last sentence takes our thoughts from
religious offerings to God, to almsgiving to men,
concerning which the son of Sirach says:

"Water will quench a flaming fire;
And almsgiving will make atonement for sins." [2]

2 Ecclus. iii. 30.

Again :

" Be not faint-hearted in thy prayer ;
And neglect not to give alms." [3]

3 Ecclus. vii. 10.

Once more :

" With Him the alms of a man is as a signet ;
And He will keep the bounty of a man as the apple of
　the eye." [4]

4 Ecclus xvii. 22.

But, at the same time, alms were not recom-
mended to be given to all alike, as the following
shows :

"There shall no good come to him that continueth to do
　evil,
Nor to him that giveth no alms.
Give to the godly man,
And help not the sinner.
Do good to one that is lowly,
And give not to an ungodly man :
Keep back his bread, and give it not to him,
Lest he overmaster thee thereby :
For thou shalt receive twice as much evil
For all the good thou shalt have done unto him.

For the Most High also hateth sinners,
And will repay vengeance unto the ungodly.
Give to the good man,
And help not the sinner." [1]

1 Ecclus. xii. 3-7.

There yet remain to be noticed a few passages in Ecclesiasticus, some of which look at almsgiving from quite a lofty point of view. Thus:

"Shut up alms in thy store-chambers [*i.e.* for beneficent purposes],
And it shall deliver thee out of all affliction :
It shall fight for thee against thine enemy
Better than a mighty shield and a ponderous spear." [2]

2 Ecclus. xxix. 12-13.

Once more :

"He that sacrificeth of a thing wrongfully gotten,
His offering is made in mockery.
And the mockeries of wicked men are not well pleasing.
The Most High hath no pleasure in the offerings of the ungodly,
Neither is He pacified for sins by the multitude of sacrifices.
As one that killeth the son before his father's eyes
Is he that bringeth a sacrifice from the goods of the poor." [3]

3 Ecclus. xxxiv. 18-20.

If now we summarize what we have gathered upon our subject from the Apocrypha, we notice first, and negatively, that we have found no passages implying that the payment of tithes and other offerings was repealed, or fell into disuse, during the period succeeding the return of the Jews from captivity, to the final destruction of their temple, or, say, during the three centuries preceding the Christian era.

On the contrary, we have met with historical incidents and allusions showing that the temple services, as restored by Ezra and Nehemiah, were continued under a regular priesthood, which suggests payment in the form of tithes and offerings from the people. The laws of the Pentateuch are still recognized as the standard of right giving. Seleucus and Heliodorus, like the kings of Babylon, contribute to the Jewish temple. Tobit is represented as paying three tithes, and Judith as dedicating her spoils of war; and all this is in harmony with the canonical books of the Old Testament.

Moreover, the Apocrypha rises to a still higher platform in the enunciation of lofty principles concerning almsgiving in general; for abundant, discriminating, proportionate giving of alms, accompanied with prayer and fasting, is strongly urged upon all. He who would keep the law is instructed to multiply offerings, none appearing in the presence of God empty-handed. The reasons given, are, that alms are pleasing to God; that, when rightly offered, they deliver from death, and purge away sin. Also, it is promised, as leading to temporal prosperity, that the Lord will recompense the liberal giver sevenfold. He is exhorted, accordingly, in every gift to show a cheerful countenance, and to dedicate his tithes with gladness.

CHAPTER VIII

TALMUDIC TEACHING ON THE FIRST AND SECOND TITHES

FROM the Talmud we get not only fuller and more detailed ideas of tithe-paying during the period between the Old and New Testaments, but we learn also how this practice was affecting the daily life of a religious Jew when Christianity appeared.

The Talmud contains the spoken or traditional law of the Jews, as distinguished from their law written. It is said by the Jews, that when God gave the written law on Mount Sinai, He delivered also to Moses, a number of precepts and explanations thereon, which were handed down by word of mouth to Joshua, to the seventy elders, to the men of the great synagogue, and so on to the great rabbis of a later period.

Whatever of truth there may be in this tradition,

it is well known that much activity was manifested in collecting precepts and decisions about the law, with comments thereon by the rabbis, in the days of the Maccabees, or, say, the second century before the Christian era, though it was not until the second century after Christ, that the rabbinical rules, interpretations, and decisions, some four thousand in number, were codified and arranged according to subjects, as we have them now.

The Talmud consists of a text called the *Mishna*, with comments called *Gemara*. The first division of the *Mishna* is on "Seeds," or matters relating to agriculture, of which the third, seventh, and eighth books respectively treat of doubtful matters connected with tithing; with the first or tithe proper, and with the second tithe.[*]

1 Chap. I. sect. 1.　In Book VII.,[1] on *Maaseroth*, or the first tithe, we find it stated as follows :

"This general rule has been handed down about the tithe : whatever serves for food, is worth keeping, and grows out of the ground, is subject to tithe: and another rule handed down is, that whatever is eatable at the beginning, as well as when fully grown, although customarily kept till it is mature, is subject to tithes, be it small or grown large. But when, in its early stages it is not an ordinary article of food, but becomes so later, it is not subject to tithe until fit to be eaten."

Section 2 determines from what time fruit becomes

---

[*] The *Mishna* has been translated into Latin by Surenhusius, and into French by Schwab. Both are before me ; but I shall attempt to translate, or in some cases to give the gist of, such sections only as are likely to serve our purpose in illustrating Jewish opinion and practice concerning tithe-paying.

subject to tithe : for instance, figs, when they begin
to ripen ; grapes, when transparent ; and mulberries,
when they turn red, etc. The next section settles
similar questions respecting black fruit generally ;
whilst section 4 names the time for tithing green
vegetables, such as gourds, cucumbers, melons, etc.

Sections 5-7 determine at what moment fruits
are considered as gathered or harvested, and so
tithable. For gourds and cucumbers it is when
the down, or bloom, has gone off, or, this indica-
tion failing, when they are collected in heaps.
Vegetables which are sold in bundles are tithable
when packed and covered up. Dried pomegranates
and raisins are tithable when heaped up ; onions
when they peel ; corn when gathered ; and wine
when the froth of fermentation has risen.

Chapter II.[1] lays down, that if a man suspected [1] Sects. 1-3.
of not paying his tithes offer figs in a public place,
one may eat them ; but if brought to the house,
they must be tithed. Again, if persons seated
before a door or shop offer figs, they may be eaten
without scruple ; but the proprietor himself, seated
at home, must pay tithe for what he has gathered.
Also, if one is carrying fruits from Galilee to
Judea, for instance, or if one is going up to Jerusalem, he may eat of them on the road up to his
destination, or on his return ; and hawkers who
sell in the towns may eat of their fruits up to the
place where they spend the night, but then they
must pay tithe.

Sections 4-8 set forth that when one says to
another, " Take this penny [or Roman *as*] and give

me five figs," they must not be eaten unless tithed ; but that a man, if giving a penny to be allowed to select ten figs, may choose and consume them one by one without tithing. In the case of workmen employed in the field, it is a general rule that when the law allows eating, the tithe is waived, but not otherwise. Again, if figs for different purposes are exchanged for each other, tithe must be paid. Rabbi Judah says, however, if they exchange figs that can be readily eaten, they must be tithed, but not if they are under process of drying.

1 Sects. 1, 3, 7-10.   Chapter III.[1] provides that when figs are placed in a court-yard to dry, all the owner's family and his servants not on board wages, may eat without tithing ; but if food is part of the servants' wages, they are not to eat [without tithing]. So, if a man working amongst olive-trees eat olives one by one, he need not tithe ; but must do so if he collects a number of olives. Similarly, if engaged to weed onions, and the workman bargain that he may eat the green leaves, he may pluck them singly and eat ; but if he gather them into a bundle, he must pay tithe.

Products placed on watch-towers, sheds, and summer-houses are exempted from paying tithes.

If a fig-tree is planted in a court-yard, one may eat now and then without tithing ; but if one gather several figs, they must be tithed. So, again, if a fig-tree planted in the yard leans toward the garden, one may eat without restriction ; but if the tree stands in the garden and leans toward the courtyard, the figs may be eaten one by one untithed, though not when several are gathered together. As for towns on the borders of Palestine, this question [of overhanging branches] is decided by the position of the trunk of the tree; but in the cities of refuge and at Jerusalem, by the direction of the branches.

The six sections of Chapter IV. provide, among other things, that he who preserves, cooks, or salts, fruits, must pay tithe; whilst he who places them underground (to keep) may eat without tithing. If children have buried figs in the field, to eat on the Sabbath, having omitted the tithe, they cannot, even on the evening after the Sabbath, eat them before the tithe is paid.

Again, if a man take olives from a basket and dip them one by one in salt, he may eat without tithing, but not if the olives have been salted already. Similarly, when leaning over a wine-press, one may drink the wine without tithing, whether mixed with warm water or cold; though some rabbis say that in either case the tithe should be paid.

By way of illustrating the minuteness to which these practices were regulated, it may be added that Rabbi Simeon, son of Gamaliel, lays it down that even little buds or sprays of fennel, mustard, and white beans, are liable to tithe.

Chapter V.[1] states that if one pull turnips or radishes to transplant in the same field, or for the purpose of gathering or taking out seed, he owes the tithe.

Moreover, as soon as the products of the land

[1] Sects. 2-4. 7-8.

have reached the period for tithing, they may not be sold to any one suspected of keeping back the tithe; nor, in the seventh year, to one suspected of non-observance of the Sabbatical year. Neither, again, ought one to sell straw in which grains of corn may be left, nor dregs of oil, nor grape-skins (for extraction of juice), to any one suspected of withholding tithes. If, notwithstanding, it should be done, tithe ought to be paid.

Even the holes of ants which may have passed a night near a heap of tithable produce are equally liable to the tithe, because it is well known that all through the night they are carrying it away to their nests.

Once more, strong garlic that makes the eyes water, the onion of Rikhta, peas of Cilicia, and lentils of Egypt; also the seeds of the slender leek, of watercress, onions, beet, and radishes—in fact, seeds that are not eaten as such, are exempt from tithe.

This may suffice for extracts from Book VII. of the *Mishna* concerning the first tithe, which contains in all forty sections; but of these I have alluded to about thirty only, thinking this will be enough to give an idea of Talmudic teaching on this part of our subject.

Let us now proceed to deal similarly with the book *Maaser Sheni*, or the Second Tithe, which has also five chapters and contains fifty-four sections. We read of the second tithe in Deuteronomy xiv. 22-7. It consisted of the yearly increase of the land, which was to be eaten with firstlings of herd and flock at the ecclesiastical metropolis; but if this place were too far from a man's home, he might turn his increase into money, and take the money to this central place of worship, and there spend it at the religious festivals.[1]

1 See p. 27.

Accordingly Chapter I. begins: They do not sell the second tithes, nor pledge them, nor exchange, nor weigh anything against them as an equivalent; neither does any one say to his neighbour at Jerusalem, "Take of my wine and give me of your oil," or the like with other products. Men may, however, give to each other reciprocal presents.

Sections 2-4 and 7 lay down that it is not permissible to sell the tithe of living cattle nor to employ the price for betrothing a wife. Also, that it is not lawful to change the second tithe for defaced money or obsolete coins, nor for money not yet in possession.

If with the price of the second tithe a man purchase a beast to serve for a peace offering, or a wild animal for a banquet, the skin is to be considered profane. Moreover, that there is not to be bought with the price of the second tithe slaves, servants, lands, nor unclean animals. If, notwithstanding, this should be done, the equivalent in value ought to be consumed at Jerusalem. So also, as a general rule, that there ought to be restored, by consuming the equivalent at Jerusalem, everything not serving for food, drink, or anointing, which has been taken from the money of the second tithe.

Chapter II. in its nine sections sets forth, among other things, that the second tithe ought to serve for food, drink, and anointing, the oil being perfumed at pleasure, but not the wine. Rabbi Simeon, however, as opposed to other rabbis, was of opinion that a man ought not to anoint himself at Jerusalem with oil of the second tithe.

With regard to money, if one should drop at the same moment ordinary coins and other coins representing the proceeds of the second tithe, what is gathered should first of all make up the amount of the tithe, and the rest should be applied to the other amount. Again, he who converts small coins of the second tithe into a shekel (for convenience of carriage) ought so to convert the whole; and if at Jerusalem one should convert a silver shekel into small money, the whole shekel should be changed into copper.

1 Sect. 1.

Chapter III.[1] sets forth that a man ought not to bid his neighbour carry fruits of the second tithe to Jerusalem, offering him as a recompense a part of the fruit; but that he should say, "Carry these to Jerusalem in order that we may eat and drink together." People might, however, make reciprocal presents.

Fruit having been brought to Jerusalem as second tithe might not be taken away again, though the money of the second tithe might. Again, fruit bought with the money of the second tithe, and which had become unclean, might be redeemed; though, according to Rabbi Judah, unclean fruit ought to be buried. Similarly, when a deer purchased with money of the second tithe had died, it should be buried in its skin. Rabbi Simeon, however, is of opinion that a man may redeem the carcase.

Chapter IV. provides that if one has brought fruits of the second tithe from a locality where they are dear, to a place where they are cheap, or *vice versa*, a man may redeem them at their price in the place of arrival, the profit, if any, going to the tithe. When one desires to redeem the second tithe at a low rate, the rate must be fixed at the cost price to a shopkeeper. When this price is well known, the valuation of a single person suffices; but if unknown, the estimates of three persons should be taken—as, for instance, in the case of wine that has begun to turn sour, deteriorated fruit, or imperfect coins.

When a man redeems his second tithe he must add one-fifth to its value. Artifice, or evasion, is so far permitted in regard to the second tithe, that a man may give money to his adult son and daughter or his Hebrew servants, engaging them for that sum to redeem the second tithe (without adding the fifth); but he may not do so by his younger children or by Gentile slaves, because their hands are, as it were, his own.

Money that is found, no matter where, is considered profane, even if one find a piece of gold among silver and copper coins; but if one find among them a fragment, even of earthenware, whereon is written the word "tithe," the whole is sacred; or, again, if one find a vase with any of the letters ק מ ד * inscribed, the vase may be considered profane.

The fifth chapter of the book on the second tithe has fifteen sections. Taking one here and there by way of illustration, we learn[1] that pious and conscientious persons deposited money during the Sabbatical year to redeem the four-year-old vines, declaring that all fruit gathered therefrom should be considered, by this money, redeemed. Also,[2] that the produce of vines of the fourth year was to be carried to Jerusalem from all suburbs within a day's journey.

Section 6 mentions that, on the eve of the Feast of the Passover, they proceed to the removing or bringing away of all legal dues. Also[3] towards the hour of the evening sacrifice, on the last day of the feast, the declaration is made :

" I have brought away the hallowed things out of mine house "[4] (which, says the *Mishna*, means the second tithe) ; " and also have given them unto the Levite" (which applies to the Levitical tithe), " and unto the stranger, to the fatherless, and the widow" (which comprises poor's tithe, gleanings, forgotten sheaves, and corners of the field)."

The *Mishna* adds that the not having carried out these precepts ought not to be an obstacle to the recitation of the formula. If, however, the second tithe has been levied before the first, the declaration ought not to be recited ; nor if a person has infringed the commandment, " I have not eaten thereof in my mourning."[5] Neither, again,

Margin notes:
Sect. 1.
[2] Sect. 2.
[3] Sect. 10.
[4] Deut. xxvi. 13.
Deut. xxvi. 14.

---

* These letters indicated, in times of persecution, the Hebrew words for sacrifice, tithe, doubtful tithe, etc.

should the declaration be made by proselytes or freed slaves, who have no share in the land.

The *Mishna* also observes that John Hyrcanus (high-priest B.C. 135) abolished the recitation of the declaration which accompanied the offering of the tithes ; adding, too, that under him none had need to seek information on the *demai* (tithe) or doubtful points of tithing.

7

CHAPTER IX

THE "DEMAI," OR DOUBTFUL TITHE

THERE is a book in the *Mishna* called *Demai*, which in point of order comes before the books on the first and second tithes, but which for our present purpose has been reserved till now.*

Chapter I. begins by naming certain things, which by reason of their trifling value are exempted from the *demai* tithe, such as inferior figs, artichokes, service-berries, shrivelled dates, late grapes, wild grapes, and buds of capers, coriander, etc.

After this it is pointed out that the *demai* tithe differs from the other tithes, because among other

---

* *Demai*, according to Maimonides (*Surenhusius*, vol. i. p. 76, col. 2), is a word signifying that about which there is a doubt whether from it should be offered gifts to God ; and he adds that it was an obligation to render 1 per cent., or a tenth of a tenth, to the priest, after which they separated the second tithe, which the owner consumed at Jerusalem. Lightfoot, on Luke xviii. 12, says : דמאי est *res dubia*. Id est, cum ignoratur, an de ea sumpta sit decima, necne. Et hæc etiam est vox composita דא מאי quid hoc ?

things, when redeeming it, a fifth need not be added,
nor need it be brought out of the house as prescribed
in Deuteronomy xxvi. 13. Again, persons in mourn-
ing might eat thereof;[1] it might not only be brought [1] Deut. xxvi. 13.
to Jerusalem, but carried away again; a small
quantity left on the road was treated as lost; it
might be given to a non-tithe payer or "a man
of the land" [that is an ignorant or uninstructed
person]; and, once more, the money received there-
for might be used for profane purposes.

Chapter II.[2] says, that he who undertakes [before [2] Sect. 2.
witnesses] to deserve universal confidence with
regard to tithes ought to be careful not only to pay
the tithe upon what he eats, but also on what he
sells, or buys to sell again to others; and he ought
not to accept hospitality at the house of a person
uninstructed in rabbinical tithe-paying [lest he
should eat of anything not tithed].

Again, he who engages to adopt the pure and
scrupulous manner of life of a companion of wise
men, ought not to sell to an uninstructed person
either soft fruit, or dry; he does not purchase of
him green products; he does not accept hospitality
of an uninstructed person, neither does he invite
such an one to his own house [because of his
communicating uncleanness even by his dress].

Retail shopkeepers[3] are not authorized to sell [3] Sect. 4.
products subject to *demai*, but wholesale dealers
may do so [it being taken for granted that owing
to the larger quantity, the purchaser will have paid
the proper dues].

Chapter III.[4] directs that he who wishes to cut [4] Sects. 2-3, 6.

the green leaves from bundles of vegetables, to lighten what he has to carry, ought not to throw the leaves away before levying the tithe thereon [so that no one, finding them, may eat unlawfully]. Again, he who buys green vegetables, and then, changing his mind, wishes to return them, must tithe them before so doing. Also, fruit found on the road may be eaten at once, but not put aside to be kept, before paying the tithe. Even he who delivers to his mother-in-law fruits to cook or prepare, ought to levy the (*demai*) tithe on what he gives to and receives from her.

In Chapter IV.[1] we read that if an "uninstructed" person adjure his companion by vow to eat with him, the companion, though not sure about his host paying tithe, may eat with him for one week, provided the host assures his guest that the *demai* tithe has been paid ; but that in the second week he must not eat with him unless the guest has paid the tithe.

Again, if a man commissions a person untrustworthy in the matter of tithes to buy fruits from some one worthy of confidence, he must not, for all that, rely on his messenger; but if the employer orders him to go definitely to such and such a person, he may then believe the messenger. Nevertheless, if after going to the person mentioned he says on his return, "Not having met the individual to whom I was sent, I went to another equally worthy of confidence," the messenger's opinion is not to be regarded as sufficient.

So also, if a traveller enter a town wherein he knows no one, and inquires, "Who is trustworthy?

Who pays tithes?" and if a man reply, "I am not considered trustworthy, but such and such a one is," the stranger may believe him.

Section 7 states: If two donkey-drivers enter a town and one of them says, " My fruits have not been tithed, but my companion's have," one ought not to take his word [because his testimony may be given by collusion].

Chapter V.[1] says that he who buys bread from a retail bread-seller ought to tithe each loaf. Again, he who buys from a poor man, or even a poor man himself who shall have received pieces of bread or fragments of fig-cake, ought to tithe each piece separately; but in the case of dates or figs the portion due may be taken collectively. [1 Sects. 4, 5, 8.]

He who buys from two places different products which have been declared untithed may levy from one purchase so much as will suffice for the other ; but notwithstanding this, it is well understood that a man ought not to sell untithed products, except in case of urgent necessity.

A man[2] may use corn bought from an Israelite to redeem corn purchased from a Gentile; or even corn from an Ethiopian ¡to redeem that of an Israelite ; or corn of an Israelite to redeem that of a Samaritan ; and similarly that of one Samaritan to redeem corn from another Samaritan, though Rabbi Eliezer condemns this last case. [2 Sect. 9.]

Chapter VI.[3] lays down, that he who farms a field for a percentage of the crop, be it from an Israelite, Samaritan, or Gentile, should divide the harvest in the presence of the landlord [without tithing]; [3 Sects. 1, 4, 8 11.]

but the tenant who farms under an Israelite ought to levy, before everything, the priestly portion. Again, if any one sell fruits in Syria, saying that they come from Palestine, the buyer pays tithe.

It would be easy to continue these curious and interesting extracts from others of the fifty-three sections into which the seven chapters of the book on the *demai* tithe is divided, and the inquiry might be extended (with a view to considering rabbinic beneficence generally) to such books as that on *Peah*, or the corners of the field to be left for the poor ; on *Terumoth*, or tribute from the crop due to the priests ; and on *Bikkurim*, or firstfruits ; but enough, perhaps, has now been presented from the Talmud to illustrate the character of its bye-laws, and to afford us various items of information concerning tithe-paying as practised during the period we are considering.

The Talmud clearly recognizes the first or Levitical tithe ; the second or festival tithe ; the third or poor's tithe ; and also appears to add a fourth or supplementary tithe of a tithe—that is, a levy of 1 per cent., for the priests, in certain cases which the Pentateuch left open to doubt.

The minuteness with which these bye-laws are elaborated, indicates the standard set before religious Jews who desired to live up to the traditional requirements of their law ; from which requirements, moreover, no class of society seems to have been held exempt, tithe-paying being thereby brought to bear on the daily life not only of the affluent and well-to-do, but of the labourer who weeded onions, the errand-boy sent to market, and the man who asked his mother-in-law to cook fruit.

Of course, it may be urged that some of the minute requirements previously mentioned are of a later date, because internal evidence connected with certain of the rules points to their belonging to the time of the Roman domination of Palestine ; but it is highly probable that a larger number of the rules were of very ancient usage.

When we consider that the whole of what is written in the Pentateuch concerning tithes is comprised in a few verses, it will be seen at once that so soon as the laws on tithe came to be put in force, a number of questions would be immediately raised as to how the law was to be carried out ; such, for instance, as to what particular seeds, fruits, or animals were to be tithed ; the age at which animals and products were to become tithable ; how far products of trifling value were to be disregarded, to what extent products of the second tithe might be consumed on the way to the ecclesiastical capital ; and many others.

Unless we are to imagine that every man was left to do as he pleased (which would mean confusion), it is reasonable to suppose that such questions would in the first place be referred for determination to Joshua, to the seventy elders, or to other competent authority. Such decisions, with other additions as time went on, would naturally be handed down by the priests and Levites, who, if only because their bread partly depended thereon, would be interested in preserving them ; and thus

many of the decrees and traditions embodied in
the *Mishna* may well have passed down as unwritten rules to the days not long before the
Christian era, when these traditions were committed to writing, thus serving as the basis for
their arrangement in the form we have them now.

These extracts, at all events, may suffice to show
that during the period between the Old and New
Testaments the practice of tithe-paying was in
full force, and carried out by many with a minuteness and conscientiousness such as cannot be traced
in the Pentateuch or in the after history of Israel
as exhibited in the remaining books of the Old
Testament.

There is, moreover, another and more important
consideration to Christians, which adds greatly to
the value of the evidence here collected, in that
we trace in the Talmud what was considered the
standard of tithe-paying and religious beneficence,
and what was received and practised among the
Jews in Palestine when Christianity appeared;
and consequently what probably was thought and
practised by most, if not all, of those Jews who
became the first heralds of the Cross.

CHAPTER X

CHRIST'S ATTITUDE AND EXAMPLE AS TO TITHING.

WE proceed in this, and the next chapter, to consider Jewish tithe-paying and religious beneficence as they were received and practised in the days of Jesus Christ; together with His example and teaching thereon.

During our Lord's ministry the population of Palestine, like that of India to-day, was ruled by Europeans, who were of a different religion from that of the natives. Tithe-paying, as we are aware, was well known to the Romans, and among this ruling class, we occasionally read of liberal-minded or pious soldiers, who favoured the Jews' religion, as in the case of the centurion at Capernaum,[1] who built the synagogue ; or of Cornelius, who prayed and gave alms that were had in remembrance in the sight of God.[2] Herod the Great, likewise, though an Idumean, rebuilt the Jews' temple.

But besides this European, or foreign, element in Palestine, there had also lived there for several centuries the Samaritans, who accepted the law of Moses, and consequently the obligation to pay tithes (as indeed they do to this day), whilst the mass of the people were Jews, who, concerning tithes and all other requirements, professed obedience to the laws of Judaism. That tithe-paying was a general practice in the days of our Lord and until the destruction of Jerusalem (A.D. 70) is plain from what Josephus (born A.D 37) says of himself in his thirtieth year :

"As to what presents were offered me, I despised them, as not standing in need of them ; nor indeed would I take those tithes which were due to me as a priest, from those that brought them."[3]

Again, he says of Ananias, the high-priest :

" He also had servants who were very wicked, who joined themselves to the boldest sort of the people, and went to the threshing-floors, and took away the tithes that belonged to the priests, by violence, and did not refrain from beating such as would not give these tithes to them. So also other high-priests acted in the like manner, as did those his servants, without any one's being able to prohibit them : so that [some of the] priests that of old were wont to be supported with those tithes died for want of food."

1 Luke vii. 5.

2 Acts x. 31.

3 Life, sect. 15.

4 Antiquities, bk. xx. ch. ix. sect. 2.

There was, however, in the condition of the Jews in our Lord's day, this great difference as compared with that of Jews under Jewish monarchs, in that being now enrolled as Roman subjects, they were not required by the law of the empire to observe the ordinances of the Jewish religion ; and hence it is not surprising if some may have availed themselves of the opportunity to evade the payment of religious dues, and became lax in the observance of tithe-paying and other religious duties.

But concurrently with this possible laxity, and perhaps provoked thereby, there had sprung up a great zeal for religion among the Jews, as manifested by three religious parties.

Of these the Essenes, who arose about the second century B.C., renounced their worldly goods, lived in communities in the desert, and greatly extolled the virtue of poverty.[1] There were also [1] Cohen, vol. ii. p. 19. the Sadducees, who, if not absolutely rejecting tradition and the unwritten law, brought them to the test of the Pentateuch, the authority of which they acknowledged ; whilst closely allied with these, there were the Pharisees, who accepted all the Old Testament writings with the rabbinical interpretations thereon, and who were exceedingly zealous for the religion of their forefathers.

The Pharisees arose about B.C. 150, and were not so much a sect as what we in England should now call a "party." Josephus speaks of their fraternity as numbering about six thousand.[2] The [2] Edersheim, Life and Times of Jesus, vol. i. p. 311. object of their association was twofold : first, to

secure extreme care and exactitude in the payment
of tithes and religious dues, and secondly, to
promote the observance in the strictest manner,
and according to traditional law, of the ordinances
concerning Levitical purity.

A candidate had to be admitted into the Pharisees' confraternity in the presence of three members.[1]
He might undertake the obligation as to complete
tithe paying without going forward to the vow
concerning purity; but he could not undertake
the latter, and supposed higher degree, without
passing through the lower.

If he entered upon the first degree only, he was
simply a *Næman*, who undertook four obligations,
namely, to tithe (1) what he ate, (2) what he
sold, (3) what he bought, and (4) not to be the
guest of an " outsider."   Having attained this
degree, he was looked upon as a person accredited,
with whom one might freely transact business,
since he was assumed to have paid on his goods
all religious dues.

If a candidate took in addition the "higher"
vow, he was called a *Chaber*, or associate, who
(in relation to the subject before us) undertook
not to sell to an outsider any substance, whether fluid
or solid; not to buy from him any such; nor to be
a guest with him, and not to entertain the outsider
in his own clothes [on account, that is, of their
possible impurity].

The Pharisees accordingly were tithe-payers *par
excellence* as distinguished from the הארץ עם (*Am-
ha-aretz*), or " people of the land," the uninstructed

[1] Edersheim, vol.
i. p. 311 ; Becho-
roth 30B.

ones, who knew not, or cared not, for the oral or unwritten law, and were looked down upon by the learned as " accursed." [1]   A Pharisee was regarded as an aristocratic, punctilious religionist; an *Am - ha - aretz* as a " heathen man and a publican." [2]

[1] John i. 49.

[2] Matt. xviii. 17.

What attitude, then, did our Lord assume in regard to the paying of tithes and religious offerings as respectively observed, or more or less neglected by these two classes of Jews?   It would be impossible that He should have been neutral; and we cannot imagine that He grew up in carelessness, or ignorance, or indifference to, this prominent feature of a Jew's religion.   In His days tithe-paying in Palestine was not only recognized, but " in the air," as witnessed by the minuteness of the directions of the *Mishna*.

Any man having a spark of religion was necessarily brought face to face with this question continually.   To buy a pennyworth of figs in the street involved also the responsibility of considering whether or not they had been tithed; and something similar had to be thought of even when a few leaves of vegetables were cut off and thrown aside to lighten a burden. [3]   No class of people, moreover, was free from the observance of these details, for they had to be remembered alike by the field labourer, the gatherer of fruit, and the errand-boy.

[3] See p. 100.

Accordingly, when our Lord's parents went up, as they did every year, to Jerusalem, and in the ordinary course of things took their second tithe, with legal and appropriate offerings, it could hardly have escaped the observation of their Divine Son that the festival tithe was regarded as sacred; that it might not be pledged nor sold on credit; and that if perchance for convenience of carriage some of it were turned into money (say at Nazareth), the coins received had to be perfect, nor might those coins be mingled with ordinary money.[1]

1 See p. 93.

When, further, it is remembered that for a wife to set before her husband untithed food was regarded as an offence sufficiently grave to warrant her divorce,[2] it will be seen that in our Lord's time, and with respect to this burning question, none could be neutral.

2 Mishna, Treatise Ketuboth, and De Sola and Raphall, p. 259.

Was Christ's position, then, as regards tithe-paying, that of an *Am-ha-aretz*, that is, one of the uninstructed? He certainly was not so regarded by His contemporaries. The multitudes not only heard Him gladly, but, quite early in His ministry, after the Sermon on the Mount, the crowds were astonished at His teaching, for "He taught them as one having authority."[3] Even in His own country, in the synagogue at Nazareth, many were astonished; and though some of them asked for the source of His learning, none of them doubted that the wisdom was there, for they asked, "What wisdom is this which is given unto Him?"[4]

3 Matt. vii. 28-9.

Mark vi. 2.

Later on, at Jerusalem, the Jews marvelled, saying, "How knoweth this Man letters, having never learned?"[5] and as it was at the beginning

5 John vii. 15.

of His ministry, "All the people were astonished at His doctrine,"[1] so it continued to its close, "for all the people were very attentive to hear Him."[2] Hence by the populace our Lord was never looked upon as "uninstructed," "not knowing the law," or in any way approaching "a heathen man or a publican." Nor was He so regarded by the learned. When only twelve years of age He surprised the doctors in the temple by His remarkable understanding and answers; and just as Josephus tells us[3] that he himself when a youth was frequently consulted by men learned in the law, so the Scribes and Pharisees sometimes consulted Jesus — not always, let us hope, in malice, but sometimes rather to discover His attitude towards what they regarded as criteria of orthodoxy. We have an instance of this when they brought to Him a woman taken in adultery,[4] quoting, as they did, the law, and inquiring for His opinion. On another occasion He was asked under what circumstances divorce was permissible.[5] Again, they asked what was the first and great commandment (that is the most essential principle) of the law,[6] and the Pharisees wished, likewise, to know when He thought the kingdom of God was coming.[7]

[1] Matt. vii. 28.
[2] Luke xix. 48.
[3] Life, sect. 2.
[4] John viii. 2.
[5] Matt. xix. 3.
[6] Matt. xxii. 36-8.
[7] Luke xvii. 20.

The foregoing are not inquiries such as educated men would put to an *Am-ha-aretz*. Such questions concerned their highest branch of learning, namely the law—the law, probably, both written and unwritten, to which again our Lord referred His inquirers. And that such questions were skilfully answered was borne witness to sometimes by expressed approval, as in the words, " Well, Master, Thou hast said the truth "[1]; and sometimes in general terms : " We know that Thou sayest and teachest rightly."[2]

It is noticeable also that the Pharisees expected to see our Lord, as a teacher, living up to a standard resembling their own. Hence they asked His disciples : " How is it that your Master eats and drinks with publicans and sinners ? "[3] And on another occasion they murmured, saying, " This Man receiveth sinners and eateth with them "[4]—things which the Pharisees expressly undertook not to do. But there would have been in this nothing to murmur at, and the questions would have been without point, had they regarded Him as one of the uninstructed or common people. They murmured because they expected Him to set what they thought a higher example.

The strongest proof, however, that the Pharisees regarded our Lord as an observer of the law, like themselves, is seen in the fact that early in Christ's ministry, " as He spake, a certain Pharisee besought Him to dine with him, and Jesus went in and sat down to meat."[5] Nor was this the only occasion on which He did so, for later on in His ministry He went into the house of one of the chief Pharisees to eat bread on the Sabbath day.[6]

Now, we remember that the Roman centurion at Capernaum was sufficiently familiar with Jewish custom to be aware that Jesus would contract ceremonial defilement by coming as a guest under

1 Mark xii. 32.

2 Luke xx. 21.

3 Matt. ix. 11.

4 Luke xv. 2.

5 Luke xi. 37.

6 Luke xiv. 1.

his Gentile roof,[1] since it was considered a breach 1 Luke vii. 6.
of the law for a Jew to keep company or be guest
with one of another nation.[2] But the fact that 2 Acts x. 28.
we find two Pharisees, one of them a chief Pharisee,
inviting our Lord to be their guest, is clear proof
that these rigid religionists did not look on Jesus
as a heathen man or a publican.

Our Lord's enemies, even, who watched His
every word, action, and behaviour in order to find
fault, never accused Him of not paying tithes
or ecclesiastical dues; and if not to pay tithe in
Athens was a sufficient handle wherewith a Greek
comedian might hold up to ridicule a rich com-
mercial statesman,[3] whose obligation to pay tithe 3 See Sacred Tenth, p. 27.
was not nearly so plainly enjoined as was the
case with the ordinary Jew, how gladly, may we
not suppose, would the enemies of our Lord
have exulted over a similar shortcoming, had they
been able to hold up Jesus to scorn, as a trans-
gressor of this command of Moses, and of its
interpretation according to the traditions of the
elders?

But let us pass on to inquire if we can learn
anything respecting our subject from our Lord's
own example. On the eighth day He was circumcized, and when the days of Mary's purification,
according to the law of Moses, were accomplished,
they brought the child Jesus to Jerusalem, to
present Him to the Lord, and " to offer a sacrifice
according to that which is said in the law of the
Lord."[4]

4 Luke ii. 21-4.

8

Mr. Sunlight's description of this ceremony as now observed by the Jews in Lemberg has been quoted,[1] and he adds :

> " Whilst watching the proceedings, I was reminded of a similar incident which happened in the life of our Lord, commonly called ' The presentation.' . . . Simeon, being no doubt one of the officiating priests in the temple, performed this rite, and that accounts for his taking up the child Jesus in his arms and blessing Him. Thus we see that the Redeemer had also to be redeemed, for it behoved Him to fulfil all righteousness."[2]

Again, when they had performed all things according to the law of the Lord, they returned to Nazareth, whence His parents went to Jerusalem every year, at the Feast of the Passover, taking up their Son also when He was twelve years old, after the custom of the feast.[3]

Here, then, we find the Evangelist careful to note that both parents and child were strictly observant of the Mosaic law ; and, in harmony with this when, later on, John hesitated about baptizing One so much greater than himself, Jesus answered : " Thus it becometh us to fulfil all righteousness."[4] So, again, during our Lord's ministry, He more than once showed His allegiance to the law, saying, for instance, to the leper healed after the sermon on the mount : " Show thyself to the priest, and offer the gift that Moses commanded "[5] ; whilst later He similarly directed the ten lepers : " Go, show yourselves to the priests."[6]

We know of only one occasion when our Lord was applied to for money, and then it was not for

[1] See p. 39.

[2] Jewish Missionary Intelligencer, March, 1903, p. 43.

[3] Luke ii. 39, 41-2.

[4] Matt. iii. 15.

[5] Matt. viii. 4.

[6] Luke xvii. 14.

a compulsory tax imposed by the Romans, but when His disciples were asked, at Capernaum, whether their Master paid the contribution for the support of the temple services. Moses, it is written, levied at God's command, for the furnishing of the tabernacle, a half-shekel for every one numbered ; also, on the return from captivity, the people charged themselves with the third part of a shekel, yearly, for the service of the house of God,[1] and it was to pay this contribution that Peter was directed to find a *stater*, or the equivalent of two half-shekels, in the fish's mouth, wherewith to pay for himself and his Master.[2]

1 Neh. x. 32.

2 Matt. xvii. 24-7 ; Edersheim, Temple, p. 47.

Concerning our Lord's personal arrangements about money, we know that though Himself a poor Man, yet He was accustomed to give to the poor.[3] He and His little company had, indeed, a purse, and Judas carried it ; but three objects only are hinted at upon which its contents were spent. At the well of Samaria we read of the disciples having gone away to buy food ;[4] and on another occasion the well-known habits of their Master left His puzzled disciples only two uses for money they could conjecture, when, the traitor having left the room, " some thought because Judas had the bag that Jesus said unto him : ' Buy what things we have need of for the feast' [which reminds us of the festival tithe], or that he should give something to the poor."[5]

3 John xiii. 9.

4 John iv. 8

5 John xiii. 29.

Hence it has been beautifully observed that the slender provision of the Lord and His little company was disposed of under a tripartite division, for

1 The Lord's Offering, p. 108. daily wants, God's ordinances, and charity.[1] Looking, therefore, at our Lord's perfect example in scrupulously keeping the law, we are left to infer that He not only paid tithes and all other religious dues, but that He probably exceeded what the law required.

CHAPTER XI

CHRIST'S TEACHING ON TITHING AND BENEFICENCE

WE now pass from our Lord's example to His direct teaching on tithe-paying and religious beneficence. Here we may observe that the Founder of Christianity proclaimed expressly, at the outset of His ministry, that He was not come to destroy THE LAW, but to fulfil it, and that whoever would do and teach the precepts of that law should be called great in the kingdom of heaven.[1]

1 Matt. v. 17-19.

In harmony with this, when a lawyer stood up and tried Him, saying, "Master, what shall I do to inherit eternal life?" the Lord replied, "What is written in the law"?[2] Besides which, we know *2 Luke x. 25-6.* that the law was invariably referred to by Him as the proper standard of godly living, and therefore (by implication, of course) the right standard of proper giving.

As for almsgiving, and religious beneficence in general, Jesus Christ laid down several broad and deep principles as foundations on which His followers might build.

"Give," He said, "to him that asketh thee; and from him that would borrow of thee turn not thou away."[1] "He that hath two coats, let him impart to him that hath none; and he that hath food, let him do likewise."[2] Again, "Give, and it shall be given unto you: good measure, pressed down, shaken together, running over, shall they give into your bosom."[3]

Another of these far-reaching principles was addressed to His apostles on the first occasion they were sent out to preach: "Freely ye have received, freely give."[4] And our Lord enunciated one other principle, which, in its own sphere, has no parallel in the literature of the world, and which, though not recorded in the gospels, seems to have been a household word among the early Christians, so that it sufficed for an apostle to enjoin upon the elders of the Church at Ephesus to "remember the words of the Lord Jesus, how He said, It is more blessed to give than to receive."[5]

Besides the foregoing exhortations on giving generally, our Lord expressly enjoined upon His followers the habit of giving as a religious duty.

"Sell that ye have," said He, "and give alms."[6]

Nevertheless, the giving was to be no mere perfunctory distribution of money, irrespective of the motive by which it was prompted. The giving

1 Matt. v. 42.

2 Luke iii. 11.

3 Luke vi. 38.

4 Matt. x. 8.

5 Acts xx. 35.

6 Luke xii. 33.

of alms and doing righteousness, in order to be
acceptable in the sight of God, was, He taught, not
to be done ostentatiously, so as to be seen by men,
but rather so unobtrusively that one's left hand
was not to know what the right hand was doing.[1] 1 Matt. vi. 1-4.
Nor was a gift to be offered on the altar by a man
at variance with his brother; but rather, the gift
should be left before the altar, and a reconciliation
be first effected."[2]   2 Matt. vi. 23.

Neither, again, was almsgiving to be done with
a view to reciprocal favours:

"When thou makest a dinner or a supper, call not
thy friends, nor thy brethren, nor thy kinsmen, nor rich
neighbours; lest haply they also bid thee again, and a
recompense be made thee. But when thou makest a feast,
bid the poor, the maimed, the lame, the blind, and thou
shalt be blessed: because they have not wherewith to
recompense thee: for thou shalt be recompensed in the
resurrection of the just."[3]   3 Luke xiv. 12-14.

As a further encouragement to such almsgiving
and righteousness, the Lord Jesus taught, in effect,
that such good deeds thus done would be taken as
done to Himself:

"I was an hungered, and ye gave Me meat: I was
thirsty, and ye gave Me drink: I was a stranger, and ye
took Me in: naked, and ye clothed Me: I was sick, and
ye visited Me: I was in prison, and ye came unto Me.
. . . Verily I say unto you, Inasmuch as ye did it unto
one of these My brethren, even these least, ye did it
unto Me."[4]   4 Matt. xxv. 35.

As for the amount, scale, or proportion in which
alms were to be devoted, no gift, Jesus implied,
could be too small, if worthily offered: for a cup

of cold water only, given in the name of a disciple, was in no wise to go unrewarded.[1]   But, whatever may be lawfully inferred as to the religious value of gifts of intrinsically small worth, it is quite clear that it was not intended as a standard for those who ought to give more; inasmuch as we have already seen that the teaching of Christ, as recorded in the gospels, enjoins an almost lavish system of beneficence.   Indeed, there seems to be no limit to the claim which Christ made upon His followers as to the consecration to Himself of their persons and their possessions, saying, " He that loveth [not merely his money, but even] father or mother more than Me is not worthy of Me: and he that loveth son or daughter more than Me is not worthy of Me."[2]

In contrast to (or shall we not say in fulfilment of?) the legal spirit of the Old Testament, which named the proportion in which men should contribute of their substance to God, Jesus Christ bade His followers to seek first and before all else God's kingdom and His righteousness, promising that all such things as food and clothing should be added to them.[3]   Moreover, they were not to lay up for themselves treasure upon the earth, but to lay up for themselves treasure in heaven.[4]   Hence when the rich young ruler asked the Lord what he should do to inherit eternal life, the answer was : " Sell all that thou hast, and distribute unto the poor, and thou shalt have treasure in heaven."[5]

If this seems to us a hard test, we may remember that it was not asking more than was implied on

1 Matt. x. 42.

2 Matt. x. 37.

3 Matt. vi. 33.

4 Matt. vi. 19-20.

5 Matt. xix. 16-21.

two other occasions, on one of which our Lord
called the people unto Him with His disciples,
and said to them all, " If any man would come
after Me, let him deny himself, and take up his
cross, and follow Me," [1] a saying that was afterwards *1 Matt. xvi. 24.*
repeated with even more stringent conditions when
there went great multitudes with Jesus, and He
turned and said unto them, " If any man cometh
unto Me, and hateth not his own father, and mother,
and wife, and children, and brethren, and sisters,
yea, and his own life also, he cannot be My
disciple." [2]
 2 Luke xiv. 25-6

It follows, then, that if a man is required to give
up, when necessary, such persons and things as
are by an ordinary person most valued of all, a
man's money may not be excepted from this general
surrender. Matthew, at all events, did not treat
such terms as merely figurative, when, called by
the Lord Jesus, " he left all, rose up, and followed
Him." [3]
 3 Luke v. 28.

But, it may be asked, did not our Lord denounce
the Pharisees? The reply is, " Yes, on several
grounds, but not as regards their tithe-paying."
When they rejected a plain command of God
such as to honour father and mother, and quoted
a traditional interpretation which allowed a man
to escape from this duty as such by saying that
his money was *Corban* (or a gift to God), this,
Christ pointed out, was making void the word of
God by reducing what was a matter of obligation
to one of free will.

In view of such perversions of scripture as this,

Jesus bade His disciples to beware of the leaven of the Pharisees, which is hypocrisy.[1] But no disapproval was expressed with the Pharisee who went up to the temple to pray, because he said, "I give tithes of all that I possess."[2] His fault lay in trusting in himself that he was righteous, and in his contempt for others.

So again, in that chapter of repeated woes, one of them reads : "Woe unto you scribes and Pharisees, hypocrites, for ye pay tithe of mint, and anise, and cummin,"[3] which is in keeping with the *Mishna*, wherein Rabbi Simeon, son of Gamaliel, was of opinion that little buds or sprays of fennel and mustard were liable to tithe.[4]

But what then ? Did the Lord disapprove of this minute tithing ? Far from it, for He expressed approval, and said, "These ought ye to have done." Besides which, it should be remembered that the eight woes pronounced upon these religionists, are prefaced by the Lord's own statement ; "The scribes and the Pharisees sit in Moses' seat. All therefore whatsoever they bid you observe, that observe and do."[5]

Here then, certainly, is expressed our Lord's approval of tithe-paying, and, up to a certain point, of the teaching of the Pharisees thereon, even when that teaching seems to have been coloured with rabbinical interpretations such as could not be so minutely deduced from the laws of the Pentateuch only.

We do well further to remember, that our Lord was conversant with certain, at least, of the traditions

[1] Luke xii. 1.

[2] Luke xviii. 12.

[3] Matt. xxiii. 23.

[4] Mishna, Maaseroth, ch. iv. sect. 6; Schwab, vol. iii. p. 182.

[5] Matt. xxiii. 2-3.

now found in the *Mishna*, for He sometimes used
its arguments in. vindication of His conduct and
teaching, as, for instance, when His disciples
on the Sabbath plucked ears of corn and rubbed
them in their hands, Jesus rebutted the charge
brought against them by quoting a maxim of the
Pharisees, "The Sabbath was made for man, and
not man for the Sabbath." [1]

1 Mark ii. 7, compared with Yoma 85B, McClintock viii. 72.

Amongst a class of men such as the Pharisees,
possessing such wide divergences of character and
views,* our Lord undoubtedly had many enemies;
but there must have been some of them with whom
He had much in common, and who were friendly,
for we are told that certain of the Pharisees (and
these seemingly with goodwill) came to warn Him
"Get Thee out, and depart hence, for Herod will
kill Thee." [2]

2 Luke xiii. 31.

We know, too, that Jesus accepted hospitality,
as we have already noticed, from a Pharisee, eating
with one at Nain,[3] and afterwards entering the
house of one of their chiefs to eat bread on the
Sabbath.[4] Besides these instances, we may reason-

3 Luke vii. 36.

4 Luke xiv. 1.

* The Talmud says there were seven varieties of Pharisees: (1) The
Shechemite Pharisee, who kept the law for what he could profit
thereby. (2) The tumbling Pharisee, who hung down his head with
feigned humility and frequently stumbled. (3) The bleeding Pharisee,
who, in order not to look on a woman, closed his eyes, and so sometimes injured himself even to incurring bleeding wounds. (4) The
Pharisee who wore a mortar-shaped cap to cover his eyes from
beholding impurity. (5) The what-am-I-yet-to-do Pharisee, who, not
knowing much of the law, and having done one thing, asked, "What
next?" (6) The Pharisee impelled by fear. (7) The Pharisee
actuated by love, who obeyed the Lord because he loved Him with
all his heart (McClintock, viii. 72, referring to Mishna-Babylon;
Sota, 22*b*: Jerusalem, *Berachoth,* cap. ix.).

ably suppose that our Lord was on intimate terms with Nicodemus, who was a man of the Pharisees, a ruler of the Jews.[1]

1 John iii. 1 ; vii. 50 ; xix. 39.

These remarks, then, may suggest, in relation to our subject of tithe-paying, that it was in matters of conduct, rather than of principle, that Jesus found so much to criticize in dealing with the Pharisees. The Pharisee who invited our Lord to dine was surprised that Jesus did not first wash, as no doubt the host himself had done, after having seen that what he was about to eat had been duly tithed. But the Lord said : " Rather give alms as you are able, and behold all things are clean unto you." * [2]

2 Luke xi. 41.

But, passing now from the Pharisees, and our Lord's teaching in connection with them, we may notice three persons, all of them large givers in proportion to their incomes, who offered to God more than the utmost requirement of the law as to tithes, and each of whom was specially commended by Christ. It looks at first somewhat hard that the poor widow of Sarepta, who possessed only a handful of meal and a little oil in a cruse, should have been called upon to contribute to the support of the Lord's prophet ; but she gave largely, and Jesus commended her as having received greater honour than all the widows who were in Israel.[3]

3 1 Kings xvii. 12.

Again, the crowds called Zaccheus the publican

* I have wondered whether our Lord had this Pharisaic tithing in mind when, after a warning against covetousness, and uttering the parable of the rich fool, Jesus added : " Seek not ye what ye shall eat, or what ye shall drink, neither be ye of doubtful mind " [that is as to tithing], but rather "sell that ye have and give alms" (Luke xii. 15, 28-9, 33).

" a sinner." But even if he were an *Am-ha-aretz*, and not instructed in rabbinical tithing, he nevertheless gave half of his income to the poor, and the Lord Jesus called him " a son of Abraham," and was a guest in his house.[1]

1 Luke xix. 9.

Yet another instance. When the Lord sat over against the treasury, and afterwards commended a certain poor widow who cast two mites therein, it was not because she paid her tenth (as did many of the rich, no doubt), nor because she paid a fourth (as the covetous Pharisees would do), neither because her *demai*, or doubtful tithe, had been paid, nor because (Zaccheus-like) she gave a half, but rather because she cast in all that she had, even all her living.[2]

2 Mark xii. 42.

How, then, shall we summarize these remarks on tithes and offerings in the days of our Lord, and His relation thereto ?

All must allow that tithe-paying was enjoined upon the Jews, by God, in the law ; and we all contend that Jesus Christ, as a Jew, kept that law to the letter ; therefore the inference seems inevitable (and we have found not a tittle of evidence to the contrary) that the Lord Jesus Himself paid tithes.[*] Nor does He appear to have expected less than this of His disciples. He knew perfectly well that a Pharisee was called upon to spend some-

---

* Here, of course, we cannot dogmatize, for we do not know what means of livelihood our Lord had at His disposal. But even if we think of Him as dependent on alms, we may remember that the *Demai* chapter of the *Mishna* directs that the poor man who received pieces of bread, or fragments of fig-cake, should tithe each piece separately. See p. 101.

thing like a fourth of his income for religious and charitable purposes, notwithstanding which, Jesus told His disciples that unless their righteousness exceeded the righteousness of the scribes and Pharisees, they should in no case enter into the kingdom of heaven.[1]

Jesus Christ did not promulgate afresh for Christians, as from a New Testament Sinai, the law against murder, or adultery, or any other law; but to show the binding and spiritual nature of the Mosaic law, and its far-reaching principles, He taught that these commandments may be broken by an angry word, or even a sinful look. Neither, again, did the Lord re-enact that His followers should pay a patriarchal tithe, a Levitical tithe, a festival tithe, a poor's tithe, a *demai* tithe, or any other; but so far was He from repealing the law concerning tithes, or lowering God's claims on property, that He set before those who would be His followers a more complete fulfilment of God's law; and an ideal more lofty by far, leaving enshrined in the memories of His hearers those remarkable words "It is more blessed to give than to receive;"[2] and proclaiming to each of His would-be followers, "Whosoever he be of you that forsaketh not all that he hath, he cannot be My disciple."[3]

1 Matt. v. 20.

2 Acts xx. 35.

3 Luke xiv. 33.

CHAPTER XII

EARLY CHRISTIAN GIVING

IN previous chapters we have brought under
review various laws relating to tithes and
offerings as recorded in the Pentateuch; after which
we looked for further light from the working of
those laws in the remaining books of the Old
Testament. In like manner, having studied in the
Gospels the example and teaching of the Founder
of Christianity in relation to tithes and religious
beneficence, we have now to investigate what
further instruction is given upon our subject by
the remaining books of the New Testament.

Fifty days after our Lord's resurrection the
Holy Spirit was sent down, and St. Peter's sermon
on the Day of Pentecost is scarcely ended when,
almost immediately, we read of the first Christians

that they devoted to the calls of their new religion, not merely one or more tenths of their property, but that each gave his all; for "all that believed were together, and had all things common; and they sold their possessions and goods, and parted them to all, according as every man had need."[1]

1 Acts ii. 44-5.

Again, in the following chapter of the same book, we see Peter and John going up together into the temple at the hour of prayer, of whom a lame man solicited alms. Peter apparently recognized at once the propriety (not to say the duty) of helping the poor; but having neither silver nor gold, he gave such as he had, and that was, in the name of Jesus Christ, to bid the lame man walk.

A commotion ensued, which led to the imprisonment of Peter and John; but so far was this from diminishing the zeal and self-denial of the newly formed body of Christians that

> "The multitude of them that believed were of one heart and soul: and not one of them said that aught of the things which he possessed was his own; but they had all things common. . . . Neither was there among them any that lacked: for as many as were possessors of lands or houses sold them, and brought the prices of the things that were sold, and laid them at the apostles' feet; and distribution was made unto each, according as any one had need."[2]

2 Acts iv. 32-5.

One of these more than princely givers was Barnabas, a Levite, a man of Cyprus by race, who, having a field, sold it, and brought the money and laid it at the apostles' feet.[3] This good example provoked probably the zeal of many, and perhaps

3 Acts iv. 36, 37.

the envy of some; for Ananias also, with his wife Sapphira, sold a possession, but kept back part of the price. They then laid the remainder at the apostles' feet,[1] as if they were giving the whole, *1 Acts v. i.* thus enacting one lie before uttering other two to cover the first—with what a sad result we know. The recorded incident, however, is instructive as showing that the wholesale giving up of property by these early believers was not compulsory, this land being regarded as their own, whether in their possession or after it was turned into money.

As believers were added to the Lord, there came also "a multitude out of the cities round about unto Jerusalem, bringing sick folks and them which were vexed with unclean spirits."[2] Nor did the *2 Acts v. 14-16.* sick appeal to the apostles in vain; for they were healed every one, and in all probability they were, in many cases, also relieved by alms.

We soon learn, in fact, that there had been a church provision made for the relief of the needy, and this is suggested by the murmuring of the Gentile Christians against the Jewish Christians, because the widows of the former had been in some way neglected at the daily ministration, or distribution, of church money or similar provision.

Upon this, the apostles, calling together the mass of the disciples, pointed out that it was not reasonable that the twelve should leave preaching and ministerial work to serve "tables"—a phrase including, no doubt, the distribution of alms; whereupon seven officers were appointed to attend

9

to this department; the church thereby recognizing it as one of her duties to care for and distribute alms to the poor and needy.[1]

1 Acts vi. 1-3.

Not that the officers of the church, however, were ready to receive money from all and every source; for when Simon Magus offered money to Peter and John, saying, "Give me also this power, that on whomsoever I lay my hands he may receive the Holy Ghost," Peter said unto him, "Thy silver perish with thee."[2] Then, we are told, the Christians throughout Palestine (that is Judea, Galilee, and Samaria) had peace, being edified; and our attention is drawn specifically to the case of Tabitha, who was reported to be full of good works and almsdeeds, such as the making of coats and garments, presumably for the poor and needy.[3]

2 Acts viii. 18-20.

3 Acts ix. 36-9.

On the death of Tabitha, Peter was called to Joppa, and Tabitha was raised to life again. After this we have an instance of Gentile giving; for whilst the apostle remained at Joppa, a vision was vouchsafed to a man in Cæsarea, Cornelius by name, a centurion of the band called the Italian cohort, a devout man, and one that feared God with all his house, who gave much alms to the people. "Thy prayers and thine alms," said the divine messenger who appeared to him, "are gone up for a memorial before God. And now send men to Joppa and fetch . . . Peter."[4]

4 Acts x. 1-5.

Precisely at the same time the apostle, whilst praying on the housetop at Joppa, saw in a vision living creatures let down from heaven, and also heard a voice saying to him, " Rise, Peter; kill, and eat. But Peter said, Not so, Lord; for I have never eaten anything that is common or unclean." [1]   Nevertheless, Peter went to Cæsarea, *1 Acts x. 9-14.* and, addressing Cornelius and his friends, said, "Ye yourselves know that it is an unlawful thing for a man that is a Jew to join himself or come unto one of another nation." [2]   Notwithstanding, *2 Acts x. 28.* they invited Peter to tarry with them certain days, which he did.

For this ecclesiastical irregularity, when Peter was come up to Jerusalem, the Jewish Christians contended with him, saying, " Thou wentest in to men uncircumcized, and didst eat with them." Whereupon Peter justifies his conduct, relating his vision, in the course of which he calmly repeats to the apostles and brethren his reply to the divine message, " Not so, Lord; for nothing common or unclean hath ever entered into my mouth." [3]   *3 Acts xi. 1-8.*

These words, read in the light of a previous chapter, [4] might suggest that Peter had been all *4 See p. 108.* his life a strict tithe-payer, because, if he had so scrupulously observed the higher law (as the rabbis deemed it) concerning ceremonial purity, and not being the guest of, or entertaining, an outsider, it goes without saying that he would have observed what they regarded as the lower vow (that is, concerning tithes), and so have paid and expended annually for religious purposes a fourth, or thereabouts, of his income.

We are not told that the apostle Peter belonged, or had belonged, to the party of the Pharisees; but in the present instance he seems to speak like one. Not, however, that the Pharisees alone were careful to avoid ceremonial defilement. The reason why the captors of Jesus would not go into the Gentile judgment hall of Pilate was that they might not thereby be rendered unclean[1]; and we read that "*all the Jews*, except they wash their hands up to the elbow, eat not, holding the tradition of the elders."[2] The words, too, of Peter to Cornelius imply that it was unlawful for *any* Jew to be guest with an outsider.

Thus far, then, we have been dealing with Christian practice and principle in almsgiving and beneficence in Palestine, among the Jews, until Peter, preaching to Cornelius, opened the door of entry to the Christian Church to the Gentiles. We read, however, "They therefore that were scattered abroad, upon the tribulation that arose about Stephen, travelled as far as Phenicia, and Cyprus, and Antioch, but preaching Christianity to none but Jews."[3]

Meanwhile, certain men of Cyprus and Cyrene spake to the Grecian Jews at Antioch, where Barnabas and Saul taught for a whole year. Here the disciples were first called Christians, the one practical feature of their Christianity mentioned, being that "the disciples, every man according to his ability, determined to send relief to the brethren that dwelt in Judea, which also they did, sending it to the elders by the hand of Barnabas and Saul."[4]

Then, Barnabas and Saul, having accomplished this labour of love,[5] went back to Antioch, where,

1 John xviii. 28.

2 Mark vii. 3.

3 Acts xi. 19.

4 Acts xi. 20-30.

5 Acts xii. 25.

not long after, certain men came down from Judea, and taught the brethren that they ought to be circumcized. A deputation, therefore, was sent to Jerusalem to the apostles and elders; and it is in connection with the conference that followed we read that some, at least, of the Jewish Christians at Jerusalem, especially those who had been Pharisees,[1] had thought it needful that the Gentile 1 Acts xv. 5. converts should be circumcized, and that they should be charged to keep (presumably in its entirety) the law of Moses, which would include, of course, spending a considerable portion of their incomes for religious purposes.

Moreover, it was not ex-Pharisees alone who were of this opinion, for, later on, we read of the Christians at Jerusalem saying to Paul, "Thou seest, brother, how many [myriads or tens of] thousands of Jews there are which believe, and they are all zealous [for the observance] of the law."[2]

2 Acts xxi. 20.

This zeal for the law no doubt included the payment of tithes, which practice was, at that very moment, in full force, presumably, by these tens of thousands of converts, and so continued for many years afterwards, as witnessed by Josephus A.D. 67.[3] 3 See p. 106. Accordingly, neither here nor throughout the Acts of the Apostles is any exception mentioned concerning tithes and offerings, as if they were obsolete, or the law concerning them rescinded.

Passing now from St. Luke's testimony in the Acts of the Apostles, to that of other writers of the New Testament, we find the author of the Epistle

to the Hebrews urging Christians "to do good
and to communicate,"[1] these words including a
duty, no doubt, as Dr. A. B. Davidson puts it,
to "impart of their substance, to minister to the
necessities of those in want or in affliction."[2] So
also St. John, in his first epistle, puts before his
readers this far-reaching question : "Whoso hath
this world's goods, and beholdeth his brother in
need, and shutteth up his compassion from him,
how doth the love of God abide in him?"[3] whilst
the apostle James asks very practically, "If a
brother or sister be naked, and in lack of daily
food, and one of you say unto them, Go in peace,
be ye warmed and filled : and yet ye give them not
the things needful for the body; what doth it
profit?"[4]

It is in accordance, therefore, with these principles, that we see the early Christians did not
stint to give for, among other things, the relief of
the needy ; and so, when Paul and Barnabas were
sent to the heathen, the one practical injunction
mentioned as laid on them was, "that we should
remember the poor; which very thing," says Paul,
"I was also zealous to do."[5]

How peculiarly zealous he was we have already
seen, in his bearing the alms of the Christians from
Antioch to the famishing brethren at Jerusalem.[6]
Moreover, this was not the last time of Paul's
acting as almoner ; for, when writing to the
Romans, this great apostle says: "I go unto
Jerusalem, ministering unto the saints, for it hath
been the good pleasure of Macedonia and Achaia

[1] Heb. xiii. 16.

[2] Bible-Class Handbook on Hebrews xiii. 16.

[3] 1 John iii. 17.

[4] Jas. ii. 15-16.

[5] Gal. ii. 10.

[6] Acts xi. 30.

to make a certain contribution for the poor among the saints that are at Jerusalem." [1]   And again, in his speech before Felix, the apostle stated that, after some years, the cause that took him to Jerusalem was to convey to his nation alms and offerings,[2] all which, together with what has been previously said, tends to show that the first Christians, whether converted from Judaism or heathenism, looked upon right giving, to say the least, as an important part of right living.

[1] Rom. xv. 26.

[2] Acts xxiv. 17.

CHAPTER XIII

ST. PAUL'S TEACHING AND PERSONAL EXAMPLE

FROM the foregoing instances of Paul's ministering to the needs of Christians, let us pass to his teaching on the subject of monetary obligations, given to the churches which he founded among the Gentiles.

In the churches of Corinth and of Galatia, when on a certain occasion money was needed for the saints (that is, apparently, the poor of the church of Jerusalem), the apostle, with a founder's authority, directed or gave order :

1 Cor. xvi. 2. "Upon the first day of the week let each one of you lay by him in store, as he may prosper." [1]

Here four things may be noticed about this method of raising a charitable fund :

1. It seems to be assumed that every one would give.

136

2. Givings were to be stored beforehand.

3. Giving was to have reference to prosperity.

4. Giving, or laying by, was to be exercised every Lord's day. And it should be observed that sometimes collections, enjoined by the apostle, were on behalf of Christians outside the churches in which the contributions were made.

Other instructions upon giving, taught by Paul to his Galatian converts, seem to occur in connection with their support of the ministry, for he says:

"Let him that is taught in the word communicate unto him that teacheth in all good things. Be not deceived; God is not mocked: for whatsoever a man soweth, that shall he also reap." [1]

1 Gal. vi. 6, 7.

In addressing the Christians at Corinth Paul entered more fully into the right of Christian ministers to the support of the faithful; [2] whilst to the Christians at Rome, his words on the subject of almsgiving may serve as a broad general principle for all churches.

2 1 Cor. xvi. 1.

"If the Gentiles have been made partakers of their [the Christian Jews'] spiritual things, they [the Gentiles] owe it to them [the Christian Jews] also to minister unto them in carnal things." [3]

3 Rom. xv. 27.

The Christians of Philippi, likewise, may be mentioned in this connection, their liberality being recognized by the apostle, who wrote that "in the beginning of the Gospel no church had fellowship with me in the matter of giving and receiving, but ye only: for even in Thessalonica ye sent once and again unto my need." [4]

4 Phil. iv. 15-17.

There were other churches where, for good reasons, Paul chose to forego personal remuneration,[1] but he did not thereby give up his right thereto; for, with the Corinthian Christians, he argues thus:

> "Have we no right to eat and to drink? . . . What soldier ever serveth at his own charges? . . . If we sowed unto you spiritual things, is it a great matter if we shall reap your carnal things? . . . Know ye not that they which minister about sacred things eat of the things of the temple, and they which wait upon the altar have their portion with the altar? Even so did the Lord ordain that they which proclaim the Gospel should live of the Gospel."[2]

Here the apostle seems to have in mind two sources of maintenance for the Jewish priesthood. The one probably included tithes brought to the storehouse of the temple,[3] and the other consisted of those portions of the sacrifices which were brought to the altar and retained by the priest,[4] as signified by the words: "They which wait upon the altar have their portion with the altar."

Some may contend, however, that the law was abrogated under the Gospel. If so, how much of the law, and in what sense? Is the law so abrogated as that we may now, at our pleasure, murder, lie, and steal?[*]

1 1 Cor. ix. 12.

2 1 Cor. ix. 4-14.

3 Neh. x. 37-40.

4 Deut. xviii. 3.

* The Rev. Watts Ditchfield, a vicar whom I know in Bethnal Green, was calling on a shoemaker, who declared he would not come to church to hear the Commandments read, for, said he, "The Ten Commandments were long ago abolished." To argue, the vicar judged to be just then undesirable; but, acting on a sudden thought, he said, "Oh! I am very glad the eighth commandment is abolished, for I am just now in want of a pair of boots, and I think these are my

Have we not already seen that Christ came to fulfil the law—to confirm it to the least iota ?[1] and fulfilling is the perfecting, not the destruction, of anything.   Hence the payment of tithes and offerings applicable to the support of the ministry, and to other religious and charitable works, is clearly the duty of Christians, unless it can be shown that Christ repealed God's law previously promulgated. And this, as Leslie writes[2]:

1 Matt. v. 17-18.

2 Divine Right of
Tithes, Toronto
edition, p. 81.

" He never did, but rather confirmed it by approving the tithe payments of the Pharisees, and by ordaining that they who preach the Gospel should live of the Gospel. Some would have the Gospel merely eleemosynary—nothing due, but all freewill offerings. But was this so in the Temple ? I trow not: for though there were freewill offerings, there were also tithes and other offerings, the withholding of which was counted as robbery. Moreover, if the ministers of the Temple were sure of at least a tenth, whilst the ministers of the Gospel are not sure of a hundredth part of some men's incomes, where is the truth or appropriateness of the apostle's comparison ? "

Besides, what was it that the Lord ordained ? That every man should give just what he pleased ? This men could do without any ordinance being issued to that end. That which leaves every man perfectly at his own liberty is no law at all ; and

---

size." Whereupon he picked up a pair as he spoke, and hurried out of the shop with the boots under his arm. The shoemaker soon followed : and never afterwards raised objections to the reading of the Commandments. (From the *Quarterly Letter of the Navvy Mission Society*, December, 1902, p. 2.) Would that all who for excuse argue that the law is abolished, and so try to evade their responsibility as to setting aside a proportion of their income for God, could be thus quickly convinced !

if every man were left thus to act, Christ ordained what amounted to nothing.*

The great apostle of the Gentiles therefore seems to lay down two great principles : one, that tithes and offerings of the faithful are due for the further-ance of the Gospel ; the other, that every one should lay up in store, on Sunday, in proportion to his income, so as to have a fund from which distribution may be made as needed : for, con-cerning the support of ministers and the support of the poor, Mr. Rigby justly says, " Both are duties, under the New Testament as under the Old, but each for a different design, and a different significance, and one should never be confounded with the other.[1]

[1] Rigby, The Tithe Terumoth P. 53.

In addition to the passages already considered, there are other points concerning Christian giving which occur here and there in the writings of the apostle Paul.

* The Rev. Richard Duke, of Stirling, Ontario, an earnest advocate of tithe-paying, in support of his conviction that the tithe law is binding upon Christians, argues thus :

1. It is a principle in jurisprudence that when the reasons which originated a law continue to operate, and there is no explicit repeal of the law, the law remains in force. And this principle appears to have the lucidity and force of an axiom. . . .

2. That which passed away was the symbolical and figurative. Tithing was neither one nor the other, but a duty issuing from the moral law, which is of perpetual force.

3. True, there is no formal re-enactment of the law of the tithe. But why should such a formal re-enactment be looked for ? The law had not become obsolete ; it was not indifferently observed. On the contrary it was conspicuously honoured in the observance. Similarly there is no formal re-enactment of the Sabbath law ; but Christians recognize the law respecting the seventh of time, and by a parity of reasoning should recognize the law respecting the tenth of substance. *The Christian Guardian*, Toronto, Jan. 13, 1904, p. 9.

The Lord Jesus led His disciples to expect hospitality, even as Martha and Mary, Joanna the wife of Chuza, Herod's steward, and Susanna, and many others, ministered of their substance unto Himself.[1] So, again, when the Lord sent out the seventy, He said: "Into whatsoever house ye shall enter . . . in that same house remain, eating and drinking such things as they give: for the labourer is worthy of his hire."[2]

1 Luke viii. 3.

2 Luke x. 1-7.

Accordingly, the Apostle Paul frequently accepted hospitality from his converts. For instance, we read that Lydia, "when she was baptized and her household, she besought us, saying If ye have judged me to be faithful to the Lord, come into my house, and abide there;" which, evidently, Paul and Silas did, since, after their imprisonment (during which the Philippian jailor was converted, and set bread before them) the two evangelists went out of the prison and entered into the house of Lydia.[3] So, again, at Puteoli, Paul and his companion found brethren, and were entreated to tarry with them seven days.[4]

3 Acts xvi. 15, 34, 40.

4 Acts xxviii. 14.

In keeping with these instances Paul urges Christians to the practice of hospitality and alms-giving; and, in the same breath with such lofty precepts as "continuing stedfastly in prayer," he adds, "communicating to the necessities of the saints, given to hospitality."[5] In fact, so full is he of this subject that, when writing to the Corinthian Christians, he breaks off in the middle of a sentence to say, "Ye know the house of Stephanas, that it is the firstfruits of Achaia, and

5 Rom. xii. 12-13.

that they have set themselves to minister unto the saints." [1]

1 1 Cor. xvi. 15.

Also to these same believers in Corinth he makes known the grace of God given in the churches of Macedonia:

"How that in much proof of affliction the abundance of their joy and their deep poverty abounded unto the riches of their liberality. For according to their power I bear witness, yea, and beyond their power, they gave of their own accord, beseeching us with much entreaty in regard of this grace and the fellowship in the ministering to the saints," after which the apostle adds, "See that ye abound in this grace also." [2]

2 2 Cor. viii. 1-4, 7.

To the Christians in Ephesus he gives the following highly practical exhortation: "Let him that stole steal no more, but rather let him labour;" and to this Christian end, not merely that he may support himself, but "that he may have whereof to give to him that hath need." [3]

3 Eph. iv. 28.

Also to Timothy, Paul says: "Charge them that are rich . . . [not to] have their hope set on the uncertainty of riches; but . . . that they do good, that they be rich in good works, that they be ready to distribute, and willing to communicate." [4]

4 1 Tim. vi. 17-18.

If next we proceed to ask for the classes of persons on whose behalf Christian giving is thus called for, we find the apostle directing, concerning ministers: "Let the elders that rule well be counted worthy of double honour, especially those who labour in the word and in teaching." [5]   And again: "Let him that is taught in the word communicate unto him that teacheth in all good things." [6]

5 1 Tim. v. 17.

6 Gal. vi. 6.

There are also the claims of the poor generally, amongst whom the Christian poor are to have the first place : " Do good unto all men, especially unto them who are of the household of faith." [1]   1 Gal. vi. 10.

Also widows are mentioned ; and that, in connection with the first information we have concerning the distribution of church bounty ; [2] whilst, in general terms, the apostle more than once mentions, as a suitable object for alms, the supplying of the necessities of the saints. [3]   2 Acts vi. 1.

3 2 Cor. ix. 1, 2, 12-15 ; Rom. xii. 13.

To these may be added the call for hospitality to strangers ; [4] helping poor relations ; [5] and assistance to foreign missionaries, " because for His name's sake they went forth, taking nothing of the Gentiles." [6]   4 Rom. xii. 13 ; 1 Pet. ii 9.

5 1 Tim. v. 8-16.

6 3 John 7.

Just as we noticed, however, from the teaching of the Lord Jesus, that true Christian almsgiving was something more than mere giving of money, so we observe several like precepts on this subject from the apostle's pen ; as, for instance, when he tells the Corinthians [7] that though he bestowed all his goods to feed the poor, and had not love, it would profit him nothing. Also he enjoins upon the Romans : " He that giveth, let him do it with singleness [or liberality]" ; [8] and Paul treats on the footing of an ordinance of God, the payment even of Imperial taxes, saying, " Let every soul be subject unto the higher powers . . . Render to all their dues, tribute to whom tribute is due, custom to whom custom, fear to whom fear, honour to whom honour." [9]   7 1 Cor. xiii. 3.

8 Rom. xii. 8.

9 Rom. xiii. 1-7.

But it is in writing to the Christians of rich,

mercantile Corinth that the apostle enlarges most concerning this duty of ministering to the saints. He praises their readiness to give, telling them he gloried thereof to the Christians of Macedonia, and that their zeal had stirred up many. The Corinthians' subscriptions, however, though promised, do not appear to have been so promptly paid; and hence, some of the brethren were sent on in advance, to make up their afore-promised bounty, that the same might be ready, as a matter of bounty and not of compulsion. [1]

1 2 Cor. ix. 1-5.

After this their spiritual father continues: "He that soweth sparingly shall reap also sparingly; and he that soweth bountifully shall reap also bountifully. Let each man do according as he hath purposed in his heart; not grudgingly, or of necessity; for God loveth a cheerful giver." [2] This he supports by a Scriptural quotation, and then proceeds to state how "the ministration of this service, not only filled up the measure of the wants of the saints, but abounded also through many thanksgivings unto God." [3]

2 2 Cor. ix. 6, 7.

3 2 Cor. ix. 12.

Such, then, were the general principles concerning monetary obligations as taught by the apostle Paul; but we may fail to appreciate them adequately unless we remember the force of his own example, for he did not preach what he did not practice, nor lay upon others a yoke which he himself would not carry.

He enjoined, indeed, that if any believing man or woman had widowed daughters, they should be relieved, rather than the Church be burdened; [4] but

4 1 Tim. v. 16.

with what perfect propriety could Paul say this, seeing that when it helped to the furtherance of the gospel, he was willing to forego even his rights of maintenance.

Moreover, in trying to gauge the mind of the apostle and his ideas on the subject generally, it should not be forgotten that Paul was both a Pharisee, yea, and the son of a Pharisee. From his youth, therefore, he had doubtless been accustomed to dedicate a fourth or more of his income to God, and we refuse to suppose that he would look at his obligations from a less honest or self-denying point of view after he became a Christian.

With all delicacy he asked the Corinthians,

"Did I commit a sin in abasing myself that ye might be exalted, because I preached to you the gospel of God for nought? I robbed other churches, taking wages of them, that I might minister unto you: and when I was present with you, and was in want, I was not a burden on any man." [1]   1 2 Cor. xi. 7-9.

And the same true servant of God could say to the elders of Ephesus, "I coveted no man's silver, or gold, or apparel. Ye yourselves know that these hands ministered unto my necessities, and to them that were with me." [2]   2 Acts xx. 34.

Can we, then, imagine, for a moment, that Paul the apostle was, as a Christian man, less zealous in the observance of his obligations in money matters, than was Saul the Pharisee in obedience to the law? Tithe-paying, indeed, was a principal factor of his former righteousness, which was under the law. But what things, then, were gain to him, those he counted loss for Christ Jesus his Lord, for whom he was ready to suffer the loss of all things ;[1] thereby reminding us of his Master's words : "Whosoever he be of you that forsaketh not all that he hath, he cannot be My disciple."[2]

Having now examined our subject in the light of the remaining books of the New Testament, this seems to be a suitable point from whence to pass under review the way by which we have traversed the entire field of revelation.

The first religious act recorded of the brothers Cain and Abel, was a recognition of their duty to offer to God a portion of their substance ; and the fact that so many early nations are known to have set apart a tenth, or more, of their property whereby to honour their gods, indicates strongly, even if historical Scriptures had been silent, that this proportion must have been taught, as a primeval law, by God[3] ; and the practice of some at least of the patriarchs is in harmony with this inference.

But however this may be, it is quite clear that one, or more, tenths of income, to be expended for religious and charitable purposes, were claimed by God of His chosen people Israel, amongst whom His laws concerning tithes would appear to have been put in operation from, at any rate, the settlement in Canaan to the time of Judah's deportation to Babylonia.

On the return of the Jews from exile, the code of the Pentateuch was still recognized as the proper standard of religious obligation ; this code,

[1] Phil. iii. 6-8.

[2] Luke xiv. 33.

[3] Sacred Tenth, ch. 1-4.

in the centuries immediately succeeding, being greatly amplified in detail by the traditional interpretations of the rabbis; so that when Christianity appeared in Palestine, tithe-paying was mixed up continuously and inseparably with almost every important act in the life of a religious Jew.

Inasmuch, then, as Jesus Christ was born at such a time, and in such a country, and in a Jewish family where the law was strictly observed, there can be no doubt that He grew up a tithe-payer; nor did His enemies attempt to charge Him with a breach of the law under this head, nor with neglect of the payment of religious or ecclesiastical dues.

In His teaching, moreover, Jesus Christ never professed to repeal, abridge, or contract the law, which He emphatically said He came not to destroy, but to fulfil. He not only expressed approval of a minute payment of tithes, which, in the whole, amounted probably to a fourth of a Pharisee's income, but told His own disciples that their righteousness ought to exceed that of the Pharisees; and, as if that were not enough, He claimed from His followers a devotion of heart, life, and property, such as should exceed the love of all that a man holds dearest on earth.

And the practice of the first Christians was in harmony with such teaching; for in some instances they gave up their possessions to a common fund; whilst in the case of the apostle Paul we see a true Christian servant content to forego, for his Master's sake, his rightful claims for remuneration, whilst exhorting those whom he addressed, that, having food and raiment, they ought to be therewith

1 Tim. vi. 8. content.[1]

It seems clear, then, in the light of revelation, and from the practice of, perhaps, all ancient nations, that the man who denies God's claim to a portion of the wealth that comes to his hands, is much akin to a spiritual anarchist; whilst he who so apportions less than a tenth of his income or increase is condemned by Scripture as a robber. Indeed, if in the days of Malachi not to pay tithe was counted robbery, can a Christian who withholds the tenth be—now, any more than then—counted honest towards God?

RIGHT GIVING IS A PART OF RIGHT LIVING. THE LIVING IS NOT RIGHT WHEN THE GIVING IS WRONG. THE GIVING IS WRONG WHEN WE STEAL GOD'S PORTION TO SPEND ON OURSELVES.

INDEX OF TEXTS ILLUSTRATED OR REFERRED TO.

GENERAL INDEX

A REVISED BIBLIOGRAPHY

ON

TITHE PAYING

AND

SYSTEMATIC AND PROPORTIONATE GIVING.

THE following bibliography was compiled chiefly of such books, pamphlets, papers, articles, sermons, etc., as were read, consulted, or referred to in writing *The Sacred Tenth.*

Since the publication of that work the list has been revised ; certain items have been omitted, and several new pamphlets added.

The list is arranged alphabetically, according to author's, editor's, or translator's names ; or, in the case of anonymous works, according to the first prominent word of the title. Each work is preceded by a number ; and at the end will be found a list of authors, with the reference numbers standing in the bibliography before their respective productions.

ABBREVIATIONS.

—— signifies repetition of preceding author's name.

[   ] Square brackets inclose the known, or supposed, author's name.

A.B.C.F.M., *American Board of Commissioners for Foreign Missions.* Secretary, Rev. S. J. Humphry, 112, Washington Street, *Chicago,* U.S.A.

A.B.M.U., *American Baptist Missionary Union,* Tremont Temple, *Boston, Massachusetts,* U.S.A.

A.B.P.S., *American Baptist Publication Society,* 182, Fifth Avenue, *New York City* ; and 1420, Chestnut Street, *Philadelphia.*

A.T.S., *American Tract Society,* 54, Bromfield Street, *Boston, Massachusetts,* U.S.A., and 150, Nassau Street, *New York City,* U.S.A.

B. & C.S.I., *Bible & Colportage Society of Ireland,* 41, Fleet Street, *Dublin.*

BLACKSTONE, *William E. Blackstone,* Oak Park, *Cook Co., Illinois,* U.S.A.

B.P.H.E., *Brethren Publishing House, Elgin, Illinois*, U.S.A.

BRIGGS, *William Briggs*, Wesley Buildings, *Toronto, Canada.*

C.G.P., *The Christian Giving Publishing Co., New York City*, U.S.A.

C.S.B., *Commission on Systematic Beneficence.* T. J. Morgan, 111, Fifth Avenue, *New York City*, U.S.A.

C.T.C., *The Churchman's Tithe Club.* Hon. Secretary, Rev. Lewis T. Wattson, 1702, North 26th Street, *Omaha*, U.S.A.

EATON, *Eaton & Mains*, 150, Fifth Avenue, *New York City.*

F. & O.C.A., *Free & Open Church Association*, Church House, Dean's Yard, *Westminster*, S.W., and 517, Locust Street, *Philadelphia*, U.S.A.

F.C.S., *Free Church of Scotland.* Printer, Frank Murray, 9, Young Street, *Edinburgh.*

G.A.C.S.B., *General Assembly's Committee on Systematic Beneficence.* Chairman, Rev. W. H. Hubbard, 156, Fifth Avenue, *New York City*, U.S.A.

G.C.C.A.E., *General Conference Commission on Aggressive Evangelism*, 150, Fifth Avenue, *New York City.*

GREEN, *The Rev. Rufus S. Green, D.D.*, Elmira College, Elmira, *New York*, U.S.A.

LAYMAN, *Thomas Kane &·. Co.*, 310, Ashland Boulevard, *Chicago, Illinois*, U.S.A.

McNAUGHTAN & SINCLAIR, Printers and Stationers, 24, West Nile Street, *Glasgow.*

MARSHALL, *Marshall Bros.*, Keswick House, Paternoster Row, E.C.

M.E.S.S.C.C., *Missionary and Evangelistic Society of the Southern Californian Conference.* F. Pearl Sigler, Field Secretary, Huntington Beach, *California.*

NELSON, *T. Nelson & Sons, London* and *Edinburgh.*

NISBET, *James Nisbet & Co.*, 21, Berners Street, *London*, W.

PARTRIDGE, *S. W. Partridge & Co.*, 9, Paternoster Row, *London.*

P.B.E., *Presbyterian Board of Education*, 1334, Chestnut Street, *Philadelphia*, U.S.A.

P.C.E., *Presbyterian Church of England.* Christian Giving Union, Henderson, Rait & Fenton, Marylebone Lane, *London.*

P.G.U., *The Proportionate Giving Union.* Hon. Secretary, Miss Watkins, Heveningham, *Yoxford, Suffolk.*

PRITCHARD, *Esther Tuttle Pritchard, Kokomo, Indiana*, U.S.A.

R.T.S., *Religious Tract Society*, 65, St. Paul's Churchyard, *London.*

S.A., *Salvation Army*, 101, Queen Victoria Street, *London*, E.C.

S.P.C.K., *Society for Promoting Christian Knowledge*, Northumberland Avenue, Charing Cross, *London*, W.C.

S.T.G., *Society of the Treasury of God.* Hon. Secretary, S. E. Gunyon, 7, Ickburgh Road, *Upper Clapton*, N.E.

STOCK, *Elliot Stock*, 62, Paternoster Row, *London*, E.C.

S.V.M.F.M., *Student Volunteer Movement for Foreign Missions,* 3, West 29th Street, *New York City,* U.S.A.

T.C.T.A.A., *Twentieth Century Tithers' Association of America,* 731, Indiana Pythian Building, *Indianapolis, Indiana,* U.S.A.

U.S.C.E., *United Society of Christian Endeavour,* Tremont Temple, 646, Washington Street, *Boston, Massachusetts,* U.S.A., and 163, West 63rd Street, *New York City,* U.S.A., and 155, La Salle Street, *Chicago,* U.S.A.

W.B.F.M., *Women's Board of Foreign Missions of the Presbyterian Church,* 53, Fifth Avenue, *New York City,* U.S.A., and 1516, Locust Street, *St. Louis, Missouri,* U.S.A.

1. **A Clergyman of Church of England.** What is Mine? What is God's? Occasional Paper No. 1. *S.T.G.,* 1888

2. **Adams, Robert.** How it Paid. *Green*

3. Address on Systematic Benevolence, by the General Assembly to the Ministers and Churches under its Care. See *How Much shall I Give?*

4. Address to Churchmen on the Duty of Giving. *C.T.C.*

5. **Adler, Hermann.** Irresponsible Wealth. *Nineteenth Century Review,* December, 1890. Leonard & Scott, *New York City*

6. **Aghadoe, Archdeacon of.** The Principles of Christian Giving. Church of Ireland Printing Co., *Dublin,* 1905

7. **Alexander, John.** Christian Stewardship. Tract. 1520, Chestnut Street, *Philadelphia,* U.S.A.

8. **Amerman, W. L.** Learning to Give : How Promoted by the Christian Endeavour Missionary Committee. Foreign Missionary Library, 156, Fifth Avenue, *New York*

9. **Anderson, Edward Pretot.** Christian Giving and Living. No. 66. *A.B.P.S.*

10. **Anderson, M. B.** The Right Use of Wealth. *A.T.S.,* 1873

11. **Angus, John.** The Financial Arrangements of Methodism. 1*d.* 26, Paternoster Row, *London*

12. **Anonymous [Davenport].** The Payment of Tithes ; or, The Lord's Portion a Tenth. D. Hobbs & Co., 231, George Street, *Glasgow*

13. **Anonymous.** Suggestions for Christian Stewards. Methodist Mission Rooms, *Toronto, Canada*

14. **A North Country Layman.** Money : What is it ? How to make it. What to do with it. Macniven & Wallace, *Edinburgh*

15. **Arnot, William.** The Race for Riches. Johnstone & Hunter, *London* and *Edinburgh,* 1851

16. **Arthur, William.** The Duty of Giving Away a Stated Proportion of our Income. *Nisbet,* 1862

17. —— Proportionate Giving. No. 256. *Eaton*

18. **Arthur, William.** The Duty of Giving Away a Stated Proportion of our Income. *How Much shall I Give ?*

19. **Ashmore, Dr. W.** The Garden of the Great King. *A.B.M.U.*

20. **Ayres, W. A.** Seven Reasons for Tithing. 20 cents per 100.
    Rev. Chas. A. Cook, Superintendent, General Commission
    on Christian Stewardship, *Bloomfield*, N.J.

21. Back to the Stones. *B.P.H.E.*

22. **Baer, John Willis.** The Tenth Legion of the United Society of
    Christian Endeavour. *U.S.C.E.*

23. —— Facts about the Tenth Legion of the United Society of
    Christian Endeavour. *U.S.C.E.*

24. **Bailey, Dr.** Loud Calls for Christian Giving. No. 60. *A.B.P.S.*

25. **Baldwin, Maurice, Bishop of Huron.** Annual Address delivered
    before the Synod of the Diocese in London, Ontario, June 16,
    1885. Advertising & Publishing Co., *London, Ontario, Canada*

26. **Ballard, Frank Otis.** Straight Lines in Church Finance.
    2 cents. Missionary Society of the Methodist Episcopal Church,
    150, Fifth Avenue, *New York City*

27. —— On Honouring God with our Substance. Price $1 per 100.
    Frank O. Ballard, 1603, Ashland Avenue, *Indianapolis,
    Indiana*, U.S.A.

28. **Barbour, Rev. Dr.** Christian Giving. Document No. 3. *C.S.B.*

29. **Barker, M. P.** Proportionate Giving. Vol. I., No. 2. *C.G.P.*

30. **Barnes, Lemuel C.** Motives instead of Enticements in Giving.
    A.B.M.U.

31. **Barrister, A.** The Universal Obligation of Tithes.
    Stock, *London*, 1901

32. **Bashford, J. W.** It Tendeth to Poverty. 75 cents per 100.
    Missionary Society of Methodist Episcopal Church, Rindge
    Literature Department, 150, Fifth Avenue, *New York City*

33. **Bass, Thomas J.** The King's Coin ; or, God's Fraction.
    Nisbet, *London*, 1886

34. **Beery, Charles O.** The Problem Leaflet. *B.P.H.E.*

35. **Bensted, B. G.** Tithe Money and Church Entertainments.
    Pulpit of the Cross, C.T.C.

36. **Berkeley, Lowry E.** The Measure and Method of Christian
    Liberality. *B. & C.S.I.*, 1877

37. **Bingham, W. P. S.** The Offertory : An Essay demonstrating the
    Superiority of Weekly Offerings at every Service to Pew Rents,
    as a System of Church Finance. The Fourth of *Four Essays on
    Free Worship and Finance.* Rivingtons, *London*, 1865

38. **Binney, T.** Money : A Popular Exposition. *London*, 1865

39. **Bishop of Ripon.** Two Addresses delivered at Diocesan Conference at Leeds. 1. The Presidential Address. 2. Systematic
    Almsgiving. A. W. Lowe, High Street, *Knaresborough*, 1891

40. **Black, William.** Congregational Finance. An Address.
David C. Clark, 23, Royal Exchange Square, *Glasgow*

41. **Blacksmith (A).** The Path to Wealth; or, Light from my
Forge.   B. F. Johnson & Co., *Richmond, Virginia,* U.S.A.

42. **[Blackstone, W. E.]** Diagram showing the Wealth of Protestant
Church Members in the United States.   30 cents per 100.
Blackstone

43. —— Investments.   *Blackstone*

44. —— Am I my Brother's Keeper? 20 cents per 100. *Blackstone*

45. Board and Tithing. Comment from *Christian Endeavour World,*
September 17, 1903.   *Boston, Mass.,* U.S.A.

46. **Boase, C. W.** Tithes and Offerings.   Clark, *Edinburgh,* 1865

47. **Bohun, W.** A Tithing Table.   1868

48. **Bolton, T. H.** The Tithe Acts.
R. D. Dickinson & Co., 89, Farringdon Street, *London,* 1886

49. **Bonar, Andrew A.** Christian Giving. A paper in *The Christian*
for July 17, 1879.   *London*

50. **Bond, B. W.** The Grace of Giving.
Printed at the Southern Methodist Publishing House,
Nashville, Tennessee, U.S.A.

51. **Bonnell, Charles B.** Articles of Association of St. Stephen's
Church.   *Manayunk* Sentinel Print, *Philadelphia,* U.S.A.

52. —— Proportionate Giving; or, Why, What, and How we should
give.   McNaughton & Sinclair, *Glasgow*

53. **Booth, General.** The Lord's Corner Guild. A New Venture for
the Missionary Field. 101, Queen Victoria Street, *London,* E.C.

54. **Bosworth, Ed. I.** The New Testament Conception of the
Disciple and his Money.   *A.B.C.F.M.,* 1902

55. Boxes for Lenten Offerings. Price 2s. for 50.   *S.T.G.*

56. **Boys, Ernest.** Money as a Talent.   *Nisbet,* 1885

57. **Brain, Belle M.** Speaker's Part. The Ministry of Money; or,
The Grace of Giving.   *U.S.C.E.*

58. —— The Ministry of Money; or, The Grace of Giving. $1.50
per hundred.   *U.S.C.E.*

59. **Broadus, John A.** Glad Giving. A Sermon. 5 cents.
Baptist Book Concern, *Louisville, Kentucky,* U.S.A., 1894

60. **Browne, T. Lloyd M.** Almsgiving. A Paper read before Rhyl
Church Congress.   Amos Bros., *Advertiser* Office, *Rhyl,* 1891

61. **Burr, Dr. E.** The Law of Christian Giving. No. 56. *A.B.P.S.*

62. **Business Man.** Conscience and System in the Stewardship of
Money. 2d.   Morgan & Scott, *London,* 1887

63. **Butler, H. E.** Systematic Almsgiving. A Paper read before
Ripon Diocesan Conference. A. W. Lowe, *Knaresborough,* 1891

64. **Butler, Samuel.** Genuine Remains. Paper entitled *The Miser,*
Vol. II., p. 341.   1759

65. Calendar of Christian Stewardship for Baptist Churches.
   47, Franklin Street, *Boston, Massachusetts*, U.S.A.

66. **Calkins, Harvey Reeves.** The Victory of Mary Christopher.
   Jennings & Pye, *Cincinnati*; and *Eaton*

67. Can all give a Tenth? From *The Life of Faith*, February 5,
   1902. *London*

68. **Candlish, Dr.** The Duty of laying by, for Religious and Charitable Uses, a Stated Proportion of our Income. *Nisbet*

69. **Capen, Samuel B.** Sunday School Offering. *A.B.C.F.M.*, 1903

70. **Carleton, George.** Tithes examined and proved to be due to
   the Clergie by a Divine Right. *London*, 1606

71. **Carnegie, Andrew.** Wealth, and the Best Fields for Philanthropy.
   Victoria Publishing Company, 179, Victoria Street, *London*, W.

72. —— The Gospel of Wealth, and other Essays.
   The Century Company, *New York*, 1900

73. **Caro, Joseph ben Ephraim.** Code Civile et Penal du Judaisme.
   Paris, 1896

74. **C. A. S. S.** Resources of the Kingdom. A Paper for Women, and
   Important Statistics for Men. *Chicago*, U.S.A.

75. Catechism [of the Catholic and Apostolic Church]. October, 1858.
   8s. per 100 net. Pitman, 140, Gower Street, *London*, W.C.

76. **Cather, Robert G.** (Edited by). The Benefactor : The Quarterly
   Journal of the Systematic Beneficence Society. *Nisbet*, 1863–73.

77. —— Origin and Objects of the Systematic Beneficence Society.
   Nisbet, 1872

78. **Chadwick, Edward W.** The Moral Effects of Charity ; or,
   Character and Almsgiving. *S.P.C.K.*, 1900

79. **Chadwick, Samuel.** Systematic Giving.
   "Animo et Fide," 18, Park Row, *Leeds*

80. **Chalmers, Thomas** (Works of). On the Love of Money.
   Discourse VIII., p. 187. *Glasgow*

81. **Chaplin, W. Knight** (Edited by). Report of Christian Endeavour
   Convention, held at Glasgow, 1898.
   Andrew Melrose, 16, Pilgrim Street, *London*

82. **Chapman, Mary S.** The Deacon's Tenth. No. 5. 50 cents
   per 100. Free to those who think they cannot pay. *Layman*

83. Chat about Proportionate Giving, A. *P.G.U.*

84. **Chetham, Humphrey.** A New Defence of Tithes : Being an
   Answer to the Legal Argument by Mr. Eagle. *London*, 1832

85. **Chisholm, James J.** The Gospel in Gold; or, The Grace of Giving.
   Presbyterian Committee of Publication, *Richmond, Virginia*

86. Christian Giving : Synod's Pastoral Letter for 1887. *P.C.E.*

87. Christian Giving Union, The. *P.C.E.*

88. Christian Liberality. 3 doz., post free, 1s. 6d.
   William Clee, Clarence Street, *Cheltenham*

89. Christian Steward, The : An Essay on the Right Appropriation of Incomes, whether derived from Business, Salaries, Wages, or other Sources ; with Specimen Accounts of Monies devoted to Religious and Benevolent Objects. See *Gold and the Gospel.*

90. Christian Steward, The. Issued quarterly by the Association of Christian Stewards. Price 25 cents a year.
F. C. Stephenson, 33, Richmond Street, West, *Toronto*

91. Christian Stewards' League, Prospectus of. *Layman*

92. Church Finance. A Dialogue between an Office Bearer and a Church Member. *Daily Journal* Office, Clayton Street, *Newcastle-upon-Tyne*, 1894

93. Church Finances. No. 1,719. *A.B.P.S.*

94. Church and the Poor. "Monthly Paper." Open Church Association, March, 1892. C7, Exchange Buildings, *Liverpool*

95. Churchman's Tithe Club. Address: *The Pulpit of the Cross*, Vol. II., No. 10, and Vol. III., No. 3, No. 10. February 27, 1897, *C.T.C.*

96. —— Membership Pledge. *C.T.C.*

97. **Clarke, Henry William.** A History of Tithes. *London*, 1891

98. **Claughton, Thomas Legh.** The Best Means of raising Local Funds in Parishes ; A Paper read at the Church Congress at Oxford. Report, 1862

99. **Clements, Jacob.** Systematic and Proportionate Almsgiving. Paper read at the Lincoln Diocesan Conference, 1892.
2*d.*, James Williamson, 290, High Street, *Lincoln*

100. **Cobb, E. M.** Won't hold Water. *B.P.H.E.*

101. **Cobweb, Caleb.** On the Giving of Tithes. The *Golden Rule*, April, 1897. *U.S.C.E.*

102. **Cohen, J.** Les Pharisiens. 2 vols. *Paris*, 1877

103. **Colford, Julian King.** The New Gospel of Wealth. *Sunday Strand*, March. *London*, 1904

104. **Comber, Thomas, D.D.** Historical Vindication of the Divine Right of Tithes. Second Edition. Parts I. and II.
London, 1682 and 1685

105. Commandment of the Law and Testimony.
Press of Society of Christian Israelites, *Ashton-under-Lyne*

106. Committee anent the Duty of Systematic Giving to the Cause of Christ, to the Members of the Free Church of Scotland.
Printed by Frank Murray, 9 and 11, Young Street, *Edinburgh*

107. Committee on Systematic and Proportionate Giving, Circular Appeal from. A Letter sent to 1,000 Ministers. February, 1903.
22, Hill Street, *Edinburgh*

108. **Common, Andrew.** An Address on the Money Question.
Hills & Co., 6, Fawcett Street, *Sunderland*

109. —— The Law of a Tenth, or Christian Giving.
Hills & Co., 188, High Street West, *Sunderland*, 1887

110. **Common, Andrew.** The Gospel of Giving.

        Hills & Co., 6, Fawcett Street, *Sunderland*, 1891

111. Consecrated Purse, A. Price ½*d*.

        Charles Brewer, 13, Perseverance Road, *Leominster*

112. **Constable, Henry.** An Essay on the Measure of Christian Liberality. See *Gold and the Gospel*.

113. Constitution of the Proportionate Giving Association of Canada [founded March 19, 1901].

114. **Cook, Charles A.** The Holy Spirit in Church Finances. No. 477.   *A.B.P.S.*

115. —— Systematic Giving : The Church's Safeguard against Nineteenth Century Evils.

    W. Briggs, 78, King Street East, *Toronto*, 1888, and *A.B.P.S.*

116. Co-operation between Young People's Societies of Christian Endeavour and the American Board.   *A.B.C.F.M.*

117. **Corbett, Dr.** How much ? A Plea for Proportion. 4*d.* per doz.

        McNaughtan

118. **Courtice, A. C.** Principles underlying Christian Giving : Proportionate and Systematic.   *Briggs*

119. **Cowan, J. F.** The Pocket-book Opener. Tract.

    Society of Christian Endeavour, *Boston*, U.S.A.

120. **Craig, A. M.** Storing.

      Turnbull & Spears, Printers, *Edinburgh*, 1903

121. **[Dalrymple, Alexander M.]** See *The Lord's Offering; or, The Exchange of the Kingdom*.

122. **Davenport, —.** The Payment of Tithes.

      D. Hobbs & Co., 231, George Street, *Glasgow*

123. **Davies, T.** The Church and its Treasury. *Weekly Storing*, 1866

124. Deaconess Worker, A. One Woman's Experience in Tithing. 20 cents per doz.   *Pritchard*

125. **De Forest, Henry S.** Giving as an Act of Worship.   *A.T.S.*

126. **Degge, Sir S.** The Parson's Counsellor : The Law relating to Tithes and Tithing.

    R. D. Dickinson & Co., 89, Farringdon Street, *London*, 1684

127. **De Sola, D. A.** *and* **Raphall, M. J.** Eighteen Treatises from the Mishna.   *London*, 1843

128. **De Winton, Wilfred S.** Church Finance. A Paper read at the Church Congress, Exeter.   Report, October, 1894

129. **D. H. S.** Biblical Finance. Pamphlet.   *Chicago*, U.S.A.

130. **Dick, Thomas.** An Essay on the Sin and the Evils of Covetousness.

    Robinson, Pratt & Co., 259, Pearl Street, *New York*, 1836

131. **Dickson, Nicholas.** The Elder at the Plate : A Collection of Anecdotes and Incidents. New Edition. 6*d*.

      Morison Brothers, *Glasgow*

132. **Dickson, Thomas S.** A Forward Movement in Christian Giving. Missionary Record of United Free Church of Scotland, 1901

133. —— Church Fairs and Bazaars. [No. 12. Talks about Christian Giving, December, 1885.]
The Christian Giver Publishing Company, *New York City*

134. —— How should a Christian Give? The Missionary Record of the United Presbyterian Church.   March, 1898

135. —— Paul's Financial Method. (Reprint of How should a Christian Give.)   *G.A.C.S.B.*

136. —— Systematic Giving. Report of Christian Endeavour Convention held at Glasgow, 1898.
Andrew Melrose, 16, Pilgrim Street, *London*, and *U.S.C.E.*

137. Discourse on the Obligation of Tithe. Delivered in Catholic and Apostolic Church, Gordon Square, October 5, 1858. Reprinted. 4*d.*   Pitman, 140, Gower Street, *London*, W.C.

138. **D. M.** Christian Giving: A Bible Study. *The Christian*, January 30.   *London*, 1902

139. **Dodge, D. Stuart.** Systematic Benevolence.
Bonnell, Silver & Co., *New York City*

140. Dollar Membership, A.   *B.P.H.E.*

141. **Drake, Mrs. E. R.** A Tithe for the Lord. Tract.
Bible House, Astor Place, *New York City*

142. Dream of Titheland, A. Tract No. 4.   *S.T.G.*, *Toronto*

143. **Drummond, Peter.** The Right Way of Giving. 1*s.* per 100.
Partridge

144. **Duke, Richard.** The Divine Law of Giving: Being an Argument in Proof that all to whom the written Revelation has come are bound by the same to tithe their Income unto God.
William Briggs, *Toronto*, 1898

145. —— Proportionate Giving. *The Christian Guardian*, January 28, 1903.   *Toronto*, Canada

146. —— Christian Stewardship. *The Christian Guardian*, January 13, March 2, and June 1, 1904.   *Toronto*, Canada

147. **Dull, W. O.** The Pay is Sure. *The Missionary Visitor*, June, 1903.   *B.P.H.E.*

148. **Duncan, William.** The Consecration of Money to the Service of God.   Aird & Coghill, 263, Argyll Street, *Glasgow*

149. **Eagle, William.** The Ancient Law of Tithes: Showing that Tithes are the Property of the Public and the Poor.
Whittaker & Co., *London*, 1871

150. **Easterby, William.** The History of the Law of Tithes in England.   *Cambridge*, 1888

151. **Eddy, Alice M.** Mrs. Pickett's Missionary Box. 4*d.* per doz.
McNaughtan

152. **Eddy, George Sherwood.** The Opportunity of the Hour; or, Christian Stewardship. *S.V.M.F.M.,* 1901

153. —— My Silver and Gold. 1*s.* *Marshall*

154. —— The Law of Christian Stewardship. Pamphlet. *Briggs*

155. **Edwards, Aubrey.** Giving to God: a Layman's View of the Matter. *S.P.C.K.*

156. **Edwards, W.** Christian Stewardship. Pamphlet.
A. McLay & Co., 6, Duke Street, *Cardiff, Wales*

157. **E[lderfield], C[hristopher].** Civil Right of Tythes.
London, 1650

158. **E. L.** The S.T.G. What is it?
Charles Cull & Son, 12 and 15, Houghton Street, *London*

159. **Emerson, F. F.** The Teaching of Christ concerning the Use of Money. *A.B.P.S.*

160. **Everett, Robert Lacey.** Tithes: Their History, Use, and Future. 6*d.* James Clarke & Co., *London,* 1887

161. Expenditure of a Christian. *Guardian,* October 30, *London,* 1901

162. **Fairgrieve, Thomas.** A Plea for the Increase of our Sabbath Offerings or Collections. Alexander Walker & Sons, *Galashiels*

163. Fancy Fair Religion. Classified Notes and Extracts. ½*d.,* or 3*s.* 6*d.* per 100. Stevenson, 9, North Bank Street, *Edinburgh*

164. **Faris, John T.** God has paid me my Salary. *Christian Endeavour World,* June 23, 1904.

165. **Faunce, W. H. P.** The Law of Sowing and Reaping. Document No. 4. *C.S.B.*

166. **Ferry, Joseph B.** Corporate Action and Systematic and Proportionate Giving in the Church of England. 1*d.*
C. Thomas, 202, High Street, *Lincoln,* 1895

167. —— The Organization of the Alms of the Church. Report of Lincoln Diocesan Conference, 1895.
Printer, James Williamson, High Street, *Lincoln*

168. —— Corporate Action and Systematic and Proportionate Giving, together with a Second Paper on same Subject. 6*d.*
Clifford Thomas, 202, High Street, *Lincoln*

169. —— Serving God in the Nation. A Sermon preached in Lincoln Cathedral, 1896. *S.T.G.*

170. —— Serving God in the Church.
Charles Cull & Son, 12 and 15, Houghton Street, *London*

171. Five Times Two is Ten. Issued by Missionary Committee.
U.S.C.E.

172. **Fletcher, George.** Obligation and Advantages of Sabbath Storing for the Lord. *Partridge,* 1865

173. **Forneret, George A.** How shall I Give? *A.T.S.*

174. **Forwell, William.** Sermon on Christian Giving.
John Durham & Son, 49, High Street, *Dundee*

175. **Foster, J. Priestley.** Fancy Fair Religion ; or, The World converting itself. Swan Sonnenschein, *London*, 1888

176. **Fox, G. Townshend.** A Sermon on Systematic Beneficence.
Nisbet, 1866

177. Freewill Offerings in Free and Open Churches. *F. & O.C.A.*

178. **French, John Abbott.** Giving in Hard Times. *P.B.E.*

179. **Fuller, Morris.** The Alleged Tripartite Division of Tithes in England. *1s.* Bosworth, *London*, 1885. *S.P.C.K.*, 1900

180. **G. A. C. S. B.** To Ministers and Members of the Presbyterian Church in Ireland. 1904

181. **G. A. K.** The Use of Money. From the *Church Missionary Intelligencer*, March, 1900. *London*

182. **Gates, Fred.** Systematic Beneficence. No. 1,237. *A.B.P.S.*

183. General Assembly's Committee on Systematic Beneficence. Document No. 31. *Green*

184. **Gibbon, Benjamin J.** The Ethics of Giving. *Congregational Church Magazine.* April, 1901

185. **Gifford, O. P.** Concerning the Collection. Price \$1.25 per 100.
Observer Publishing Co., *Greensburg, Indiana*, U.S.A.

186. —— Tithing a Duty.
Delaware Avenue Baptist Church, *Buffalo, New York*

187. **Gilpin, W.** The Widow's Mite. A Sermon. From a volume entitled *Gilpin's Sermons.*
Thos. Hatchard, 187, Piccadilly, *London*, 1855

188. Give ; or, What the Bible says about Almsgiving. Pamphlet.
S.T.G. and *S.P.C.K.*

189. Giver, The Conscientious. 25 cents per 100.
General Committee of Christian Stewardship :
Rev. Chas. A. Cook, Superintendent, *Bloomfield*, N.J.

190. Giving. Price *9d.* per doz. *Marshall*

191. Giving Alphabet. *American Bible Society's Record*, Vol. XLIII. p. 42. *New York*

192. Giving, What ? 2 cents. *W.B.F.M.*, November, 1897

193. **Gladstone, W. E.** Mr. Carnegie's *Gospel of Wealth :* A Review and a Recommendation. *Nineteenth Century.*
London, November, 1890

194. —— *Record*, p. 211. *London*, March, 1898

195. **Glassford, James.** Covetousness brought to the Bar of Scripture.
Nisbet, 1837

196. **Gledstone, J. P.** Should Christians make Fortunes ?
Headley Bros., 14, Bishopsgate Street Without, *London*

197. Gold and the Gospel. The Ulster Prize Essays. By HENRY CONSTABLE, JAMES MORGAN, ROBERT SPENCE, JOHN ROSS.
Nisbet, *London*, 1877

198. Good Point, A. *A.B.M.U.*

199. **Gordon, A. J.** God's Tenth. *A.B.M.U.*
200. —— Dr. Gordon's Letter. *A.B.M.U.*
201. Grace of Giving, A Few Texts on. *F. & O.C.A.*
202. Grace of Giving, The. *Chronicle of London Missionary Society*, July, 1905.
203. **Granger, Francis.** The Divine Plan of Church Finance. Baker Jones & Co., Printers, *Buffalo, New York*, U.S.A., 1891
204. **Grove, Henry.** Alienated Tithes in Appropriated and Impropriated Parishes, commuted or merged under Local Statutes and the Tithe Acts, together with all Crown Grants of Tithes, from Henry VIII. to William III. For the Author's subscribers. *London*, 1896
205. **Grubb, Percy H.** Giving. *Church Missionary Gleaner*, February, 1902. *London*
206. **Guilliam [*or* Guillim], Sir Henry.** Edited by C. ELLIS. Acts, etc., relating to Tithes. Second Edition. 4 vols. 1825
207. **Guirey, George.** How to Open the Windows of Heaven. No. 79. *A.B.P.S.*
208. **Hale, Sir Matthew.** Edited by T. THIRLWALL. Works: The Great Audit; Concerning my Wealth and Temporal Subsistence. Vol. II., p. 288. 2 vols. *London*, 1805
209. **Hamilton, James.** Tithes. *S.P.C.K.*
210. —— An Inquiry into the Principles of Church Finance in Ancient and Modern Times. (The third of *Four Essays on Free Worship and Finance*.) Rivingtons, *London*, 1865
211. **Hamilton, Kate W.** Thanksgiving Ann. (Getting and Thanksgiving.) 4d. per doz. *Layman;* and *McNaughtan*
212. **Hamlin, Teunis S.** Business Principles in the Administration of Churches. *The Independent*, 130, Fulton Street, *New York*. September 19, 1901
213. **Hancock, T.** The Puritan and the Tithes. S.P.C.K., *London*, 1905
214. **Hannah, John.** The Law of Christian Giving. *Wesleyan Methodist Magazine*, February and March, 1865. Wesleyan Conference Office, City Road, *London*
215. **Harris, John.** Mammon, or Covetousness the Sin of the Christian Church. Thos. Ward & Co., Paternoster Row, *London*, 1837
216. **Harris, Sidney.** Modern Methods of Raising Money: Are they Scriptural? *Joyful News* Depôt, *Rochdale*
217. **Hartley, W. P.** The Use of Wealth. Thos. Law, Memorial Hall, *London*, 1902
218. **Havergal, Frances Ridley.** Kept for the Master's Use. Chapter VII., "Our Silver and Gold," p. 99. Nisbet, *London*
219. **Hay, E. H.** Tenths a Minimum. Price 1d. or 50 for 3s. *S.T.G.*

220. **Hebblethwaite, A.** Concerning the Collection.

            11, City Road, *Manchester*

221. **Helm, Stephen.** I must Draw the Line Somewhere. *A.B.P.S.*

222. **Hewitt, C. E.** Results of Christian Giving.   *A.B.P.S.*

223. **Heylyn, Peter.** Historical and Miscellaneous Tracts. *The Right and Patrimony of Tithes*, p. 163.   *London*, 1681

224. **Hibbert, G. K.** Systematic Giving. Report of Christian Endeavour Convention, held at Glasgow, 1898.

        Andrew Melrose, 16, Pilgrim Street, *London*

225. **H[ills], A[gnes].** Offerings to God.

     Chas. Cull & Sons, 12 & 15, Houghton Street, Strand,
                                  London

226. **H. N. T.** Will a Man rob God ? St. Bartholomew's Church Tracts, No. 20. ½d. Charles Taylor, 23, Warwick Lane, *London*

227. —— What does your Religion cost you ? St. Bartholomew's Church Tracts. No. 35. ½d.

             Taylor, 23, Warwick Lane, *London*

228. **Hobson, John C.** Systematic Giving in its Relation to Missions, September, 1885. No. 9. Talks about Christian Giving.

      The Christian Giver Publishing Co., *New York*, U.S.A.

229. **Hobson, J. P.** What we Owe. From a Lawyer's Standpoint.

   Presbyterian Committee of Publication, *Richmond, Virginia*

230. **Hohannes, John.** A Sermon on Tithes.   *A.B.C.F.M.*

231. **Holmes, Mrs. F. L.** Christian Stewardship. Tract.

      Frank Wood, 252, Washington Street, *Boston*, U.S.A.

232. **Horsefield, F. J.** Systematic Giving.

             Christian Endeavour Times, London

233. **Hovey, Dr. Alvah.** The Christian Teaching of Old Testament Offerings. Document No. 1.   *C.S.B.*

234. —— How and Why should I Give ? No. 33. The price of this tract, and all others of this size, is at the rate of $1 for 1,000 pp. in any quantity, and the Society prepays the postage. *A.B.P.S.*

235. How ? and How Much ?.   Tract Repository, *Dublin*

236. How can I Find Out ?   *B.P.H.E.*

237. How Much shall I Give ? A Series of Tracts on the Subject of Systematic Benevolence. [By WILLIAM ARTHUR, D. V. SMOCK, W. S. PLUMER.]   *P.B.E.*

238. How to Give the Bible Way. No. 12.   *P.B.E.*

239. **How, W. Walsham.** The Best Investment.   *F. & O.C.A.*

240. **H. T.** Christian Giving. An Address delivered before the Y.M.C.A.   Bible House, Pilgrim Street, *Newcastle-on-Tyne*

241. **Hubbard, J. G.** Church Finance. A Paper read at the Church Congress at Oxford.   Report, 1862

242. **Hughes, H. Price.** Irresponsible Wealth. *Nineteenth Century Review*, December, 1890.   *New York City*

243. **Hughes, H. Price.** The Duty of Systematic Giving. *The Home Messenger*, February, 1903.

> Horace Marshall & Son, Temple House, Temple Avenue, *London*

244. **Humphrey, S. J.** Mammon *versus* Missions. No. 567. *A.T.S.*

245. —— For His Sake. 60 cents per 100. Issued by Rev. A. N. Hitchcock, District Secretary. *A.B.C.F.M.*, January, 1894

246. —— A Story of the Bees. $1 per 100. *A.B.C.F.M.*

247. **Hunter, J. E.** Pay, Pray, and Prosper. Pamphlet. *Briggs*

248. **Hurlin, William.** What is Christian Giving? No. 54. *A.B.P.S.*

249. Illustrations of Giving that entails Sacrifice from Members of a Working-class Congregation. 2d. per doz. *McNaughtan*

250. Is it Right? Supplement to *The Missionary Visitor*, February, 1904. *Elgin, Ill.*, U.S.A.

251. Israel's Heaps. 5 cents per doz. *W.B.F.M.*

252. Jack Randolph's Tithe. *S.T.G.*

253. **Jenkins John.** Christian Giving. Illustrated and enforced by Ancient Tithing. A Discourse preached in St. Paul's Church, Montreal, 1881.

> Mitchell & Wilson, Printers, St. Peter Street, *Montreal*

254. **Jerdan, Charles.** The Counterfeit in Church Finance and Christian Giving. *Nisbet*

255. **Jessop, A.** Before the Great Pillage. *London*, 1901

256. **Jessup, E.** Tithing : Its Origin and Warrant. *Canadian Presbyterian Record*, September, 1894.

257. **Jones, G. Edwardes.** History of the Law of Tithes in England. 2s. *London*, 1888

258. **Jones, J. S.** Proportionate Giving and Offertory Development. 1s. 6d. per 100. *F. & O.C.A.*

259. **Joyce, James Wayland.** The Doom of Sacrilege, and the Results of Church Spoliation. *London*, 1886

260. **Judd, O. B.** Good Stewards. No. 49. *A.B.P.S.*

261. **Kane, Thomas.** See *Layman*.

262. **Kelsey, H. S.** Warning against Covetousness. In *Sermons on the International Sunday School Lessons for* 1878, *by the Monday Club*. Henry Hoyt, *Boston*, 1878

263. Key to the Situation. General Missionary and Tract Committee. *Elgin, Ill.*, U.S.A.

264. **Kidder, Charles.** The Systematic Giver. *S.T.G.*, Toronto, 1886

265. **Kilpatrick, J. H.** Liberal Giving : How to Secure It. No. 42. *A.B.P.S.*

266. **King, G. A.** The Use of Money. *Students and the Missionary Problem*, p. 160.

> Student Volunteer Missionary Union, *London*, 1900

267. **Langdon, William Chauncy.** Reform in Church Finance. Reprinted from *American Church Review*, October, 1883.
E. and J. B. Young & Co., Cooper Union, Fourth Avenue, *New York City*, 1884

268. **Langford, William S.** Christian Beneficence : Its Motive, Measure, and Method.
Thomas Whittaker, 2 & 3, Bible House, *New York City*

269. **Lansdell, Henry.** Russian Central Asia. 2 vols. *London*, 1885

270. ——The Sacred Tenth ; or, Studies in Tithe-giving Ancient and Modern. 2 vols. 16 shillings. *S.P.C.K.*, 1906

271. ——The Tithe in Scripture. Half a crown. *S.P.C.K.*, 1908

272. **Latham, H. J.** God in Business.
John Menzies, Copthall Avenue, *London*, 1905

273. **Layman [Thomas Kane].** The Pew to the Pulpit. ~~40 cents~~ per 100. ~~Free to those who cannot pay.~~ *Layman*

274. —— What we Owe, and Why we Owe it. $1 per 100, or ~~$8 per 1,000. Free to those who cannot pay.~~ *Layman*

275. —— What we Owe, and How to Pay it. No. 2. Revised Edition. ~~$1 per 100. Free to those who cannot pay.~~ *Layman*

276. —— What we Owe, and the Results of Paying it. *Layman*

277. **Lay Member of the Church of England [J. M. Kemble ?].** Pamphlet on Historical Remarks upon the Supposed Antiquity of Church Rates, and the Threefold Division of Tithes.
London, 1837

278. Leaflet No. 1, The Example of the Heathen. No. 2, The Example of the Saints. No. 3, Firstfruits : A Lost Means of Grace. No. 4, Tithes : A Lost Means of Grace. No. 5, Offerings : A Lost Means of Grace. No. 6, A Royal Priesthood. *S.T.G.*

279. **[Leakey, Caroline W.]** God's Tenth. *1d.*
Shaw & Co., 48, Paternoster Row, *London*, E.C.

280. **Lees, Harrington C.** The Arithmetic of Heaven.
C.M.S. House, Salisbury Square, *London*

281. **Le Feuvre, Amy.** Jill's Red Bag. *R.T.S.* [1903]

282. **Leslie, Charles.** The Divine Right of Tithes.
London, 1700, and (reprint) *Toronto*, 1884

283. **Liddell, Edward.** The Poverty-stricken Clergy. A Paper read at the Church House, Westminster, June, 1893 *1d.* *S.T.G.*

284. List of Books and Tracts on the Subject of Christian Giving. Free Church of Scotland Reports. No. 32. *Nisbet*

285. Literature of Christian Giving and Systematic Beneficence.
A.B.P.S.

286. **Livesey, H.** Charity and its Relation to Temporal Prosperity. Price 3*d.* *Partridge*

287. **Locke, Charles Edward.** Tithing as a Christian Duty.
H. H. Otis & Sons, Buffalo, *New York*

288. **Locke, Charles Edward.** Young People and Scriptural Giving. Price 50 cents per 100.

> Missionary Society of the Methodist Episcopal Church, Rindge Literature Department, 150, Fifth Avenue, *New York*

289. **Long, Thomas S.** Systematic Giving. *Assembly Herald.* U.S.A. Presbyterian Church, March, 1901.

> 237, Dock Street, *Philadelphia*, U.S.A.

290. Lord's Money. The. Leaflet. *S.T.G.*

291. Lord's Money, The. A Symposium. *The Assembly Herald*, March. 1328, Chestnut Street, *Philadelphia*, U.S.A., 1905

292. Lord's Offering ; or, The Exchange of the Kingdom [by ALEXANDER M. DALRYMPLE] and the Church's Exchequer [by ALEXANDER M. SYMINGTON]; Essays on Systematic Beneficence. Andrew Elliot, *Edinburgh*, and *Nisbet*, 1877

293. **M. A.** Unpleasant Questions. 3*d.* per doz.

> Brown, 42, Hanover Street, *Edinburgh*

294. **Mackay, Dr.** Christian Giving : An Address to the Members of the Presbyterian Church of England.

> Henderson, Rait, & Fenton, Marylebone Lane, *London*

295. **Magruder, J. W.** The Way it Works. Tract.

> Rindge Literature Department, 150, Fifth Avenue, *New York City*

296. —— What a Local Church has done. Price 50 cents per 100.

> Missionary Society of Methodist Episcopal Church, Rindge Literature Department, 150, Fifth Avenue, *New York*

297. **Manley, G. T.** System in Giving. Article in C.M.S. Summer School Report, 1904.

> C.M.S., Salisbury Square, *London*

298. **Manning, Cardinal.** Irresponsible Wealth. *Nineteenth Century Review*, December, 1890. *New York City*

299. **Margöschis, A.** A Magnificent Offering from Tinnevelly. *The Gospel Missionary*, October, 1901.

> Society for the Propagation of the Gospel, *London*

300. **Mather, Mrs. James.** The Sanctification of the Tenth.

> *Woman's Home Missions*, U.S.A.

301. **McCabe, Mrs. H. C.** The Lord's Tenth. From the *Lutheran Missionary Journal*, November, 1903.

> 1424, Arch Street, *Philadelphia, Penn.*, U.S.A.

302. **McClintock, John**, *and* **Strong, James.** Cyclopædia of Biblical, Theological, and Ecclesiastical Literature. 12 vols.

> *New York City*, 1878 and 1894

303. **M. D.** Christian Giving : A Bible Study. *The Christian*, January 30, 1902. *London*

304. Memorial and Thankoffering. *The Pulpit of the Cross*, Vol. II., No. 11. *C.T.C.*

305. **Mentzer, W. H.** Giving for the Lord's Work, No. 82. *A.B.P.S.*

306. **M[errick], J. Vaughan.** Worship without Offerings Incomplete. Publication No. 30. *F. & O.C.A.*

307. —— Endowments for Churches. No. 45. *F. & O.C.A.*

308. Methodist Branch Papers, Nos. 1, 2, 3. Hon. Secretary, Rev. J. Nicholson, Golden Square, *Bendigo.*
Spectator Publishing Co., *Melbourne*

309. **M. E. W.** Godly Thrift for Favoured England. *S.T.G.*

310. **Meyer, F. B.** The Stewardship of Money. ½*d.*
Partridge ; and Fleming H. Revell Co., *New York City*

311. **Middleton, R.** What do I Give, and Why?
Jarrold & Sons, 10 and 11, Warwick Lane, *London*, E.C.

312. —— Faith, Methods in the Use of Money. *Go Forward,* November, 1904.
Y.W.C.A., 26, George Street, Hanover Square, *London*

313. **Miller, A. W.** The Law of the Tithe and of the Freewill Offering, and of Almsgiving, etc.
Printed at Presbyterian Publishing House, U.S.A., 1873

314. **Miller, D. L.** The Brethren or Dunkers.
General Missionary and Tract Committee, *Elgin, Ill.,* U.S.A.

315. **Miller, E. L.** How Estimate the Tithe.
Observer Publishing Co., *Greensburg, Indiana,* U.S.A.

316. **Mitchell, Arthur.** Giving made Easy. *The Message and Deaconess Advocate,* Vol. XII., No. 5.
Oak Park, *Chicago,* U.S.A., May, 1896

317. **Mitchell, Thomas.** Christian Beneficence, with Reference to Proportionate Giving. Kelly, 2, Castle St., *London* [1905]

318. —— Christian Beneficence.
Edwin Dalton, 48-50, Aldersgate Street, *London*, 1905

319. **M. J. F.** What the Bible says on Giving. Our Giving Series, No. 8. Envelope Edition. ½*d.* *Partridge*

320. **Mohler, John E.** Opportunities for Giving. *The Missionary Visitor,* June, 1903. *B.P.H.E.*

321. **Moir, John.** Christ's Stewards. The Bible Plan for Christian Giving. 1*d.* *Nelson*

322. —— Storing for God. The Bible Plan for Christian Giving. 1*s.* per doz. *Nelson*

323. —— Debtors to God, not Givers. The Tithe still due to God. ½*d.* *Nelson*

324. —— The Scriptural Establishment and Endowment of the Church. *Nelson,* 1896

325. —— Christian Stewards. 1 cent.

326. **Moncrieff, J. Forbes,** Edited by. Christian Giving. Classified Notes and Extracts. ½*d.*
Andrew Stevenson, 9, North Bank Street, *Edinburgh*

327. **Moncrieff, J. Forbes.** Every One of You. Giving for the Cause of Christ. 1*d.* Andrew Stevenson, 9, North Bank Street, *Edinburgh*

328. —— Giving Better than Getting.
Andrew Stevenson, 9, North Bank Street, *Edinburgh*

329. —— Giving and Withholding ; or, How to Get and How to Lose a Blessing. Our Giving Series, No. 2. 1*d.* *Partridge*

330. —— How, When, and Why ? An Address to the Young on Giving for the Cause of Christ. 1*d.*
Oliphant, Anderson & Ferrier, *Edinburgh* and *London*

331. —— Our Collectors and their Work. 1*d.* *Partridge*

332. —— Our Giving : What it is and What it Ought to Be. New and enlarged edition. *Partridge* [1902]

333. —— Tracts on Christian Giving. Nos. 1–8. 1*d.* each, or published together as *Our Giving.* *London*

334. **Montagu, Richard.** Diatribæ upon the First Part of the Late History of Tithes. 1621

335. **Moore, D.** Do you Believe the Bible ? *S.T.G.*

336. **Moore, Melville M.** Support the Parish. 1 cent.
James Pott & Co., 14 and 16, Astor Place, *New York City*, 1892

337. **Morehouse, H.L.** A Message for the Hour. Document No.2. *C.S.B.*

338. **Morgan, G. Campbell.** Studies in Malachi ; or, Wherein have we robbed God ? Morgan & Scott, *London*

339. —— The Christian and his Money. *Illustrated Missionary News*, July, 1903. *London*

340. **Morgan, James.** The Scripture Rule of Religious Contribution ; or, In what Proportion should a Believer in Revelation dedicate his Property to the Cause of God ? See *Gold and the Gospel.*

341. **Morse, L. L.** Consecration of Wealth. Address at Methodist Œcumenical Conference, 1901. *Methodist Times*, p. 684, September 19. *London*, 1901

342. MSS. in British Museum on Tithes are indicated in Class Catalogue of MSS. as *Church History*, vol. i. pp. 401–9.

343. **Müller, George.** Christian Giving. ½*d.* *Partridge*, 1879

344. —— On Giving. An extract from the 24th Report of the New Orphan Houses, Bristol. *Partridge*

345. —— The Privilege of Giving as taught in Scripture. *Partridge*

346. **Munro, Mrs. Geo.** Proportionate Giving. 1 cent.

347. **Murphy, Thomas.** Sustain the Great Enterprise. Document No. 3. *G.A.C.S.B.*

348. **Murray, Andrew.** Money : Thoughts for God's Stewards. *Marshall*

349. —— The Poverty of Christ. 1*d.*
S.A.G.M., 14A, Lingfield Road, *Wimbledon*, S.W.

350. **Neff, James M.** By the Year or by the Dollar—Which ? *The Missionary Visitor*, February, 1904. *B.P.H.E.*

351. **Noble, W. B.** Christian Giving. 3s. per 100. *R.T.S.*

352. **Noel, F. A. D.** Systematic and Proportionate Almsgiving. A Paper read before the Wakefield Diocesan Conference, October, 1892. 1d. *S.T.G.*

353. **Norris, Edward S.** The Impropriation of Tithes. Price 6d.
Eyre & Spottiswoode, *London*, 1905

354. Notes on Giving. *Missionary Herald*, 1904. *A.B.C.F.M.*

355. **Ober, C. K.** A Larger Life. *S.V.M.F.M.*

356. —— Money a Spiritual Force in the Kingdom of God.
S.V.M.F.M., 1903

357. **O'Brien, Colonel.** The Layman's Point of View.
Orillia Packet Printers, *Canada*

358. **Offertory Alms.** Pamphlet No. 75. *F. & O.C.A.*

359. **Offertory Rubric, The.** 1s. 6d. per 100. *F. & O.C.A.*

360. **Ogden, Mrs. U.** The Grace of Liberality. *Briggs*

361. On Giving. From *The Australian Churchman*, November 7, 1903. *Sydney*, N.S.W.

362. **O. P. J.** My Rich Religious Experience. 10 cents. per doz. *Pritchara*

363. **Osborne, Henry.** Giving. *G.A.C.S.B.*, 1881

364. **Osborne, John.** Tythes: An Indictment against Tythes, etc. 1659

365. **Palmer, A. T.** Generousness. Price 1d.
James Clarke & Co., 13-14, Fleet Street, *London*, 1900

366. **Pangborn, Ada L.** The Windows of Heaven Open. No. 4, *Talks about Christian Giving*, April, 1885. *C.G.P.*

367. **Pansy.** The Pocket Measure.
Lothrop Publishing Co., *Boston*, U.S.A.

368. **Parker, Joseph.** Scattering and Withholding.
The City Temple, London, 1871

369. —— The Theology of Money. *The City Temple, London*

370. —— The Working Church : An Argument for Liberality and Labour. *Nisbet*, 1857

371. Path to Wealth. With Introduction by Bishop (now General Superintendent) Carman. See *Blacksmith, A.*

372. **Pearse, Mark Guy.** Mister Horn preaches on the Great Hurt.
Eaton

373. —— Mister Horn and his Friends.
Wesleyan Methodist Book Room, *London*

374. —— A Homily of Mister Horn upon Giving.
Wesleyan Methodist Book Room, *London*

375. **Pearson, Anthony.** The Great Case of Tithes. 1754

376. —— The Great Cause of Tithes truly stated, etc., by J. M.
London, 1730-62

377. **Pearson, Hugh.** Systematic Beneficence. A Paper read before the Warminster Clerical Meeting.
Thomas Danks, 4 and 9, Crane Court, *London*

378. **Pentecost, George T.** Systematic Beneficence. When and How to Give.
A. D. F. Randolph Co., 103, Fifth Avenue, *New York City*, 1897

379. Personal Consecration to Christ. The Great Duty of the Present Age. 3 cents.
W. W. Waters, Superintendent Presbyterian Publication Rooms, 198, Penn Avenue, *Pittsburgh, Penn.*, U.S.A.

380. Personal Experiences of Christian Giving. [The Lord's Treasury Series, No. 4.] *4d.* per doz. *McNaughtan*

381. **Pierson, A. T.** Why and How shall I Give? *Experience*, No. 90, June, 1903. *Partridge*

382. —— New Incentives to Giving. From *New Acts of Apostles*.
Nisbet

383. —— Bible Plan of Giving. No. 53.
American Home Missionary Society, Bible House, *New York*

384. —— The Lord's Teachings about Money. Price *1d.*
Mildmay Mission to Jews, Central Hall, Philpott Street, *London*

385. **Pigou, Francis.** Almsgiving, Ancient and Modern. A Sermon. 3rd Edition. T. Thatcher, College Green, *Bristol*

386. **Pike, J. G.** Christian Liberality in the Distribution of Property.
R.T.S., 56, Paternoster Row, *London*, 1836

387. **Pitt, Henry A. S.** The Free-Will Offering Scheme. 4th Edition. Price *4d.*
R. Journet, 10, Great Western Road, Paddington, *London*

388. **Platt, S. H.** The Christian Law of Giving. *Eaton*

389. **Plumer, W. S.** The Great Giver. See *How Much shall I Give?*

390. Pocket, Conversion of the. *P.G.U.* [1905]

391. **Pocock, Charles A. B.** Why Give? or, A Public Confession as to the Right Motives for Proportionate Giving. *S.T.G.*

392. **Pope, C. J.** The Pastor and Systematic Giving. No. 112. *A.B.P.S.*

393. Practical Plan, A. 14, Beacon Street, *Boston, Mass.*, U.S.A.

394. **Price, Annie N.** Giving or Getting. A Letter in *The Christian*, September 21, 1893. *London*

395. **Price, Thomas.** The Case for Tithes simply Stated in a few Notes. E. Pearce, *Journal* Office, High Street, *Rhyl*, 1887

396. **Prideaux, Humphry, Dean of Norwich.** An Award of King Charles the First settling Two Shillings of the Pound out of the Rents of Houses in Norwich, etc. *London*, 1707

397. —— Directions to Churchwardens . . . to which is added a Compendium of the Law of Tithes, pp. 119–56. *London*, 1813

398. —— Original and Right of Tithes. *Norwich*, 1710

399. **Priest, A.** Our Priests and their Tithes. *London*, 1888

400. Principles and Methods. Synod Paper.
G. W. Chisholm, *New Glasgow, Nova Scotia*, 1888

401. **Pritchard, Esther Tuttle.** Catalogue of Literature on Christian Beneficence, September, 1895. 3 cents.
Mrs. Flora P. Mills, *Knightstown, Indiana*, U.S.A.

402. —— Suggestions for the Introduction of Proportionate and Systematic Giving Methods.
Miss J. B. Haines, *Cheltenham, Penn.*, U.S.A.

403. —— Stewardship and Proportionate Giving. Women's Missionary Society of the Methodist Church, Canada. 5 cents.
Room 20, Wesley Buildings, *Toronto, Ontario*

404. —— Systematic Giving and the Lord's Portion. *The Message and Deaconess World.* 240, Clinton Avenue, *Oak Park, Ill.*, U.S.A., 1902

405. —— Tithing *versus* Entertainments. Leaflet. Women's Temperance Publishing Association. The Temple, *Chicago*

406. Prize Essays on Free Worship and Finance. Four Essays by Rev. T. P. BROWNING, Rev. S. H. SAXBY, Rev. J. HAMILTON, Rev. W. P. S. BINGHAM. Rivingtons, *London*, 1865

407. Proportionate Giving for the Support of Foreign Missions. *The Mission Field*, May, 1903 *London*

408. Proportionate Giving ; or, Why we should Give, and in what Manner. No. 6. *Layman*

409. Proportionate Giving ; or, Why, What, and How we should Give ? 5d. per doz. *McNaughtan*

410. Prospectus of the Proportionate Giving Union. 3d. per doz. *P.G.U.*

411. **Rankine, W. H.** The Christian Virtue of Giving. *The Church of Scotland Home and Foreign Mission Record*, February, 1899.
42, Hanover Street, *Edinburgh*

412. Reasons for contributing Liberally in the Weekly Offertory to the Church's Support. Publication No. 3. *F. & O.C.A.*

413. **Reid, J. M.** The Ring of the True Metal ; or, the Divine Law in respect to Property. No. 255. *Eaton*

414. Report of the Committee anent the Duty of Systematic Giving to the Cause of Christ. To the Members of the Free Church of Scotland. 1875, 1880, 1882, 1883. *F.C.S.*

415. Report of Committee anent the Duty of Systematic Giving to the Cause of Christ, May, 1894. No. 34. *F.C.S.*

416. Report of the Committee on Organisation and Development of the Work of the Commission. Bulletin No. 1. *C.S.B.*

417. Reports I.—VII. of the Society of the Treasury of God, 1885 and onwards. *S.T.G.*

418. Report of Special Committee on Systematic Beneficence Appointed by General Assembly of Presbyterian Church, U.S.A.
Green, 1892

419. **Rhodes.** Scriptural Giving.
Aug. Wiebusch & Son Printing Company, *St. Louis, Missouri*, U.S.A., 1898

420. **Richardson, Peter.** The Duty and Privilege of Christians in Connexion with the Support of the Ordinances of the Gospel.
Nisbet, 1857

421. **Riddle, James W.** Systematic Giving. A Working Plan.
A.B.P.S.

422. **Rigby, N. L.** Ten Cents on the Dollar; or, The Tithe *Terumoth.*
The Tenth Club Publishing Co., *Los Angeles*, U.S.A., 1895

423. **Rivier, Theophile.** Christian Liberality. Translated from the French. Simpkin, *London*

424. **Robartes, Foulke.** The Revenue of the Gospels is Tythes, due to the Ministrie of the Word, by that Word.
Cambridge, 1613

425. **Robinson, Charles S.** Theory of Stewardship. Document No. 8. *G.A.C.S.B.*

426. **Robjohns, Henry T.** The Need and Method of Sabbath Storing for God. *Partridge*, 1865

427. **Roe, Henry.** The Place which Religious Giving is Meant to Occupy in the Christian Economy.
Bradford Bros., Chapel Street, *Sherbrooke*, Canada, 1880

428. **Rooke, F. H.** God's Tenth. Binding, Reasonable. *S.T.G.*

429. —— Rules for Giving to the Weekly Offertory. *F. & O.C.A.*

430. —— Systematic Almsgiving. A Paper written for the Rochester Diocesan Conference, April, 1890. *3d.* *F. & O.C.A.*

431. —— To Get or to Give. Why do we go to Church? *S.P.C.K.*

432. **Ross, John.** The Christian Weekly Offering; or, The Scriptural Principle and Rule of Self-assessment in the Dedication of Property. See *Gold and the Gospel.*

433. —— The Certainty of Weekly Offering; or, The Inquirer Directed *Stock*

434. —— The Lord's Portion stored on the Lord's Day. *London*

435. —— Storing for God, and Giving to God. *Stock*

436. —— The Best for the Lord. A Sermon.
Blackie & Co., *Glasgow*

437. —— *The Weekly Offering Record.* Quarterly. *Stock*, 1865-75

438. **Ross-Lewin, G. H.** Lord Scudamore: A Loyal Churchman and Faithful Steward of God's Bounty. Price *3d.*
St. Giles' Printing Company, Raeburn House, York Place,
Edinburgh, 1900

439. **Rumfitt, Dr. C.** Bible Method of Giving. *3d.* *Marshall*

440. —— Downright Stinginess: is it true? is it I? *2d.*
London Jews Society [1905]

441. **Sallmon, William H.** Systematic and Proportionate Giving. Young Men's Christian Association.
3, West Twenty-ninth Street, *New York City*, U.S.A., 1902

442. Salvation Army. The Tenth League. *S.A.*
443. **Sayce, A. H.** Patriarchal Palestine. *London*, 1895
444. **S. C. A. S.** Resources of the Kingdom. A Paper for Women. Proportionate Giving Pledge. *Pritchard*, U.S.A.
445. **Schaeffer, J. G.** The $\frac{1}{10}$ of All. No. 5. Talks about Christian Giving. The Christian Giver. *New York City*
446. **Schauffler, A. F.** Money. 5 cents. *S.V.M.F.M.*
447. **Schürer, Emil.** History of the Jewish People in the time of Jesus Christ. Emoluments of the Priesthood. Division II. Vol. I. p. 230. T. & T. Clark, *Edinburgh*, 1890
448. **Schwab, Moïse.** Le Talmud de Jerusalem. *Paris*, 1878
449. **Scott, J. R.** The Primitive Rule of Giving. *A.B.P.S.*
450. **Scott, Robert S.** The Grace of Christian Liberality.
Aird & Coghill, 263, Argyll Street, *Glasgow*, 1884
451. **S. D. H.** [A business man.] Biblical Finance. *Chicago*
452. —— The King's Portion. *Chicago*
453. **Selborne, Earl.** Ancient Facts and Fictions concerning Church and Tithes. 8vo, 7*s*. 6*d*. Macmillans, *London*, 1888
454. **Selden, John.** The History of Tythes. *London*, 1618
455. **Seymour, James Cooke.** Christ the Apocalypse. [Chapter on Wealth and its Uses : Law of Giving.] *Eaton*
456. —— The Gifts of the Royal Family ; or, Systematic Christian Beneficence—its Nature and Need.
W. Briggs, 70 and 80, King Street, East, *Toronto*, 1888
457. **Shaver, M. A.** Ten Reasons for Tithing. *Briggs*
458. **Shelton, O. Don.** Higher Ideals of Christian Stewardship. Second edition. *S.V.M.F.M.*, 1901
459. **Sheppard, W. J. L.** The Grace of Giving. Article in First C.M.S. Summer School Report, 1904.
C.M.S., Salisbury Square, *London*
460. Short Catechism of Tithes, A. Tract No. 5. S.T.G., *Toronto*
461. **Sloan, Walter B.** The Grace of Giving. 1*d*.
Morgan & Scott, 12, Paternoster Buildings, *London*, E.C.
462. **Smith, Asa.** Giving out of their Deep Poverty. Document No. 4. *G.A.C.S.B.*
463. **Smith, Edward Everett.** Christian Stewardship. *Green*
464. **Smith, G. L.** Giving as God directs. No. 6. Talks about Christian Giving. *C.G.P.*, 1888
465. **Smith, Hugh C.** Book of Remembrance. Win One Series. No. 3. Price 8 cents. *G.C.C.A.E.*
466. **Smith, Mrs. S. T.** "O. P. J." Women's Board of Missions of the Interior. 53, Dearborn Street, *Chicago*, U.S.A.
467. **Smith, Sir George.** Perils of Wealth. Essay at Methodist Œcumenical Conference, 1901. *Methodist Times*, p. 684, September 19. *London*, 1901

468. **Smith, Wemyss.** God's Way for Christian Giving. Church Series, No. 8. $2 per 100. 3 cents each.
Rev. Wemyss Smith, St. Matthew's Church, Bloomington, *Illinois*, U.S.A.

469. **Smith, W. Robertson.** Lectures on the Religion of the Semites. *Edinburgh*, 1889

470. **Smock, D. V.** Systematic Benevolence. See *How much shall I give?* Second (revised) edition, 1894. *P.B.E.*

471. **Smyly, E. S.** The Grace of Giving.
Church Missionary House, Salisbury Square, *London*, E.C.

472. So many Calls. *Eaton*

473. So many Calls. ½d. *Partridge*

474. **Soames, Werner H. K.** Proportionate Giving.
The Record, June 26, *London*, 1896

475. Some Abominations of Modern Church Finance. Tract No. 6.
S.T.G., *Toronto*

476. **South, Robert.** Sermons on Covetousness. Nos. 46 and 47. Vol. III. p. 287. *Oxford*, 1823

477. **Spelman, Sir Henry.** Larger Treatise concerning Tythes.
London, 1728

478. —— The History and Fate of Sacrilege. Fourth edition, with an Appendix bringing the Work up to the present date, by the Rev. C. F. S. WARREN. *London*, 1895

479. —— History and Fate of Sacrilege. Edited by SAMUEL J. EALES, D.C.L. Hodges, *London*, 1888

480. **Speer, Robert E.** Systematic Giving. From *Memorial of H. T. Pitkin*, p. 89. Fleming H. Revell Co., *New York City*

481. **Speer, William.** God's Rule for Christian Giving. A Practical Essay on the Science of Christian Economy. *P.B.E.*

482. **Spence, Robert.** The Jewish Law of Tithe. A Guide to Christian Liberality. See *Gold and the Gospel.*

483. **Spencer, Dwight.** Church Finance. *A.T.S.*

484. **Spufford, H. T.** The Law of Christian Giving.
Rev. H. T. Spufford, *New Bushey, Watford*

485. **Spurgeon, C. H.** A Cheerful Giver beloved of God. Sermon No. 835. Passmore & Alabaster, *London*

486. **Stanton, Mrs.** Thank-Offerings. 10 cents per doz. *W.B.F.M.*

487. Star of Oblation. *S.T.G.*

488. **Stewart, E. B.** The Tithe.
Winona Co., *Chicago*; and *Winona Lake, Indiana*, U.S.A.

489. —— The Tithe Covenant Plan for Financing the Kingdom of Christ. *Layman.*

490. **Stewart, T. C.** Systematic Beneficence; or, The Tithing System in the New Testament Church. A Sermon to be had of the Author. 1231, South 58th Street, *Philadelphia*, U.S.A.

491. **S[tock], E.** The Ministry of Money. *Church Missionary Inte.ligencer*, February, 1890. Salisbury Square, *London*, E.C.

492. Storing and Obtaining. A Quarterly Magazine 1888 to April 1901 ; and onwards, as *The Lord's Portion*, to 1905 [in progress]. 6*d.* per doz. *P.G.U.*

493. **Strickland, A. B.** Tithing in the Modern Church. Price $1.50 per 100. *Observer* Publishing Company, *Greensburg, Indiana*

494. **Strong, Josiah.** Money and the Kingdom. 2 cents. *A.T.S.*

495. **Strong, Robert.** The Farmer's Tithe-box. Leaflet. Society of Friends Foreign Missionary Union in America.
Cheltenham, Penn., U.S.A.

496. **Stuart, E. A.** The Spiritual Standard of Giving. *Students and the Missionary Problem*, p. 153.
Student Volunteer Missionary Union, *London*, 1900

497. **Stubbs, C. W.** Some Principles of Almsgiving. *The Church Monthly*, January, 1903 *London*

498. Suggestions for Christian Stewards. Methodist Rooms, *Toronto*

499. Suggestions for the More Godly Laying Aside Weekly Offerings according to 1 Cor. xvi. 2. Price 1*s.* per 100.
Charles Brewer, Holly Mount, *Leominster* ; also
H. J. Raymond, 16, Paternoster Square, *London*

500. **Surenhusius, Gulielmus.** Mischna : sive totius Hebræorum juris. *Amstelodami,* 1698

501. **Sutton, M. H.** Proportionate Giving. Letters to the Editor of *The Record,* June 22, etc. *London*

502. **Swartz, William P.** The Financial Problem. Document No. 10. *G.A.C.S.B.*

503. **Symington, Alexander M.** The Church's Exchequer. See *The Lord's Offering.* Andrew Elliott, *Edinburgh*

504. —— Why, How, and When to Give. *Nisbet,* 1880

505. System in Religious Offerings. Bulletin No. 2. *C.S.B.*

506. Systematic Beneficence. No. 31. *Green*

507. Systematic Beneficence, the Commission on, submits to the Churches the following with reference to Plans of Giving. Bulletin No. 3. *C.S.B.*

508. Systematic Giver. Paper of the [Canadian] Society of the Treasury of God. *Toronto*, November, 1886, and January, 1888

509. Systematic and Proportionate Giving. Correspondence in the *Record,* September, 1887. *London*

510. Talks on Tithes : Why Pay Them ? *S.P.C.K., London*

511. **Taylor, William.** What the Bible says about Giving. No. 429. *A.T.S.*

512. Temporal Side of Christian Giving. The Lord's Treasury Series, No. 3. 4*d.* per doz. *McNaughtan*

513. Tenth Band. Missionary and Tract Committee, *B.P.H.E.*

514. Tenth Legion, Enrolment Blank of the.
John W. Baer, 646, Washington Street, *Boston*, U.S.A.

515. Texts on the Grace of Giving. *F. & O.C.A.*

516. **T. H.** Christian Giving. *6d.* doz. Bible House, Pilgrim Street, *Newcastle-on-Tyne*

517. Thanksgiving Ann. *4d.* per doz. *McNaughtan*

518. [**Thompson (Th.)**]. Tithes Indefensible ; or, Observations on the Origin and Effects of Tithes, etc. *York*, 1795

519. **Thorndike, Herbert.** The Church's Right to Tithes, as found in Scripture [written about 1659]. Works, vol. VI. pp. 3-18. Library of Anglo-Catholic Theology. Parker, *Oxford*, 1856

520. **Thorold, A. W.** On Money. Dodd, Mead & Co., *New York*

521. Tied Hand Unloosed by Tithing. *M.E.S.S.C.C.*

522. **Tillesley, Richard.** Animadversions upon Mr. Selden's *History of Tythes.* Second edition. *London*, 1621

523. Tithe, A Discourse on the Obligation of. Pitman, *London*

524. Tithe Conference. Responsive Reading. *M.E.S.S.C.C.*

525. Tithe Covenant. *M.E.S.S.C.C.*

526. Tithe Primitive, The. *S.T.G.*

527. Tithe Scriptural, The. *S.T.G.*

528. Tithes, First-Fruits, Offerings, Gifts : All commanded by God. *M.E.S.S.C.C.*

529. Tithing from a Business Man's Standpoint. From *The Ambassador* of the Presbyterian Church, III., April 11, 1903. *Chicago*

530. Tithing. Is it Christian ? *Present Truth*, July, 1904. *London*

531. Tithing the Command of God. *M.E.S.S.C.C.*

532. **Totten, J. W.** Giving to God's Cause. *Briggs*

533. **Townley, Adam C. W.** The Sacerdotal Tithe. *New York*, 1855

534. **Townley, Frances E.** My Experience ; or, Why I Tithe my Income. 20 cents per doz. *Pritchard*

535. Town Vicar, A. How the Blessing came. *2d.* nett. *Marshall*, 1897, and Jarrold & Sons, *London* and *Norwich*

536. **T. R.** An Odour of a Sweet Smell. *1d.* *Marshall*

537. **Treleinie, P. H.** Undeceiving People in the Point of Tithes.

538. **Trumbull, H. Clay.** The Law of the Tithe. United Presbyterian Men's Movement, 616, West North Avenue, *Alleghany*, P.A.

539. **Tucker, A. Bernard.** Almsgiving. *Church Bells*, December 24, 1903. *London*

540. **Tweedie, W. K.** Man and his Money : Its Use and Abuse. Nisbet, *London*, 1856

541. **Two Clergymen.** Anti-Mammon ; or, An Exposure of the Unscriptural Statements of " Mammon." *Nisbet*, 1837

542. Two Missionary Funds of the Young People's Society of Christian Endeavour. Central Presbyterian Church. *U.S.C.E.*

543. Tythes. An Essay concerning the Divine Right of Tythes. By the Author of *The Snake in the Grass.* 8vo. 1700

544. Tythes. The Countrey's Plea against Tythes, etc. *London*, 1647

545. Uncle Ben's Bag. How it is never empty. *Partridge*, 1872

546. **Underhill, T. Edgar.** Tithes and Offerings. A Paper read before Worcester Diocesan Conference.
T. Edgar Underhill, M.D., *Barnt Green, Worcestershire*

547. **Underwood, R. A.** Will a Man rob God? Price 10 cents.
Pacific Press Publishing Company, *Oakland, California*

548. **Uhlhorn, Dr. Gerhard.** Christian Charity in the Ancient Church. Translated from the German.
Scribner's Sons, *New York*, 1883

549. **Unsworth, William.** Loving and Giving.
Wesleyan Conference Office, 2, Castle Street, City Road,
London

550. **Vicar of Clewer.** Tithes and Offerings. ½d.
Thomas E. Luff, 69, Peascod Street, *Windsor*

551. **Vox Clamantis.** The Getting and Spending of Money. Public Morality, No. 5.
James Clarke & Co., 13 & 14, Fleet Street, *London*

552. **Waffle, Albert E.** Christianity and Property: An Interpretation. *A.B.P.S.*, 1897

553. —— Giving to the Cause of Christ. Why should I Give? No. 43. *A.B.P.S.*

554. —— Is it a Good Investment? No. 40. *A.B.P.S.*

555. —— Leakage in Beneficence. *A.B.M.U.*

556. **Wakefield, Bishop of.** The Best Investment. *F. & O.C.A.*

557. **Waterworth, J.** [Translated by.] Canons and Decrees of the Council of Trent. *London*, 1848

558. **Watkins, E. A.** The Gift Bag. Thoughts and Suggestions on Proportionate Giving. 6d. per doz. *P.G.U.*

559. —— How to Give. 6d. per doz. *P.G.U.*

560. —— Storing to Give. 3d. per doz. *P.G.U.*

561. —— [Edited by.] *Storing and Obtaining.* A Quarterly Paper on Storing for God's Cause, and Obtaining from God's Hand. 1888 and onwards as *The Lord's Portion.* 6d. per doz. *P.G.U.*

562. —— Two-fold Storing. A Few Words to Young Men and Maidens. 3d. per doz. *P.G.U.*

563. —— The Churchman's Tithe Club. *Omaha*, U.S.A. *C.T.C.*

564. Weekly Free-will Offering Scheme, at Emmanuel Church, Paddington; Books and Printing for.
R. Journet, 14, Great Western Road, *London, W.*

565. **Weekley, W. M.** Getting and Giving; or, The Stewardship of Wealth.
United Brethren Publishing House, *Dayton, Ohio*, 1904

566. Week's Wages to Missions, A.

    American Board, 14, Beacon Street, *Boston*, U.S.A.

567. **W. E. M.** Godly Thrift for Favoured England. 1*d.*   *S.T.G.*

568. **Weisley, J.** Christian Stewardship. No. 34.   *Green*

569. **Wells, Amos R.** The Tenth Legion. 2 cents.   *U.S.C.E.*

570. **Wesley, John.** Sermon 50. The Use of Money. Works, vol. vi., p. 124.   *London*, 1829

571. —— Sermons : (1) The Danger of Riches ; (2) Riches ; (3) The Danger of Increasing Riches.

572. **Whallon, E. P.** Is all your Income your Own ?   *Layman*

573. What Christians Owe to Christ.   *M.E.S.S.C.C.*

574. What do I Give ?   S.A.G.M., 17, Homefield Road, *Wimbledon*

575. What shall I Give unto the Lord ?   *S.T.G.*

576. What the Bible says on Giving. No. 8. $\frac{1}{2}$*d.*   *Partridge*

577. **Wheeler, C. H.** Ten Years on the Euphrates. (Chapter X. Tithe-Giving Revival.)

    American Tract Society, 150, Nassau Street, *New York*

578. **Whitaker, Joseph.** Practical Guide for the Successful Working of the Weekly Offering in a Christian Church. 1*d.*   *Stock*

579. **Whitcomb, Harry.** Tithing from a Business Man's Standpoint. 75 cents per 100.   E. L. Miller, *Peru, Indiana*, U.S.A.

580. —— Tithing a Religious Duty.   *Shelbyville, Indiana*, U.S.A.

581. **White, Greenough.** The Theology of Giving.

    Domestic and Foreign Missionary Society of Protestant Episcopal Church, U.S.A., 281, Fourth Avenue, *New York*, 1900

582. **Whitehead, Bp. Cortlandt.** The Privilege and Utility of the Tithe.   Stevenson & Foster Co., *Pittsburg*, U.S.A.

583. Why Churches should be Free. Leaflet.   *F. & O.C.A.*

584. Why? "Christian Stewardship." Methodist Mission Rooms, *Toronto*

585. **Williams, Mrs. M.** Proportionate Giving.   *W.B.F.M.*

586. **Willmott, Mrs. J. B.** Proportionate Giving. Tract.

    46, Bond Street, *Toronto, Canada*

587. **Willmott, M. B.** Proportionate Giving. An Exercise. *Briggs*

588. **W. J. C.** Tithes, etc., of all the Sects and Churches. Part I.

    Barnicott & Son, Fore Street, *Taunton*, 1887

589. Word about our Finance, A. *Foreign Field*, p. 24, 1904.

    Methodist Publishing House, 2, Castle Street, City Road, *London*

590. Worship of God by Offerings. No. 20.   *Green*

591. **Wyckoff, J. F.** The Christian Use of Money.   *A.T.S.*

592. **Wylie, James A.** The Gospel Ministry : Duty and Privilege of supporting it.   *Nisbet*, 1857

593. **Wylie, W. T.** The Christian Giver. No. 313.   *P.B.E.*

594. **Young, William.** Systematic Giving the Secret of Successful Church Finance. 1*s.* per 100.   *B. & C.S.I.*

595. —— Giving to God.   Archer & Sons, *Belfast*

LIST OF AUTHORS,

WITH REFERENCE NUMBERS TO THEIR WORKS IN THE FOREGOING BIBLIOGRAPHY.

Lightning Source UK Ltd.
Milton Keynes UK
UKOW07f2324240817
307810UK00002B/83/P